HOLA
RANGER

HOLA RANGER

MY JOURNEY THROUGH THE NATIONAL PARKS

DAVID VELA

Author at Grand Teton National Park, 2019
Vela Family Photo

FOREWORD

by Robert G. Stanton
15th Director of the National Park Service
(first African American Director)

INTRODUCTION

by Fran P. Mainella
16th Director of the National Park Service
(first female Director)

DEDICATION

To Melissa
my wife and loving partner in my journey
through the national parks

To Christina, Anthony, and Amelia
my children and my inspiration

*To Xavier, Issaac, Noah, Mariah, Nathaniel,
Gabriel, and Kingston*
my grandchildren and legacy

To Raymond and Mercedes
my parents whose decision to explore our
national parks changed my life

To all of my Latino colleagues
thanks for your example, encouragement,
and support

ACKNOWLEDGMENTS

Throughout my journey through our national parks, there were many individuals who encouraged and supported my dream of one day wearing the "green and gray" of the National Park Service.

I will always be grateful to my parents and siblings, a high school sweetheart, a high school assistant librarian, an American war hero, a businessman and philanthropist, and several NPS directors (to name a few) for their inspiration, guidance, and support.

More later regarding my high school sweetheart and a national war hero. As for the high school assistant librarian, Mrs. Betty Bergstrom worked in the Wharton High School Library and was my source of information in the late 1970s on everything involving the National Park Service. During that time, all we had by way of career information in our public libraries were publications, magazines, and encyclopedias as computers were in the realm of science fiction.

Although there was more information available on being a state game warden, there was little information available to feed my appetite for data on national park rangers. However, Mrs. Bergstrom was always willing and able to do what she could to satisfy my hunger for information while in high school, and I will always be grateful.

I first met John L. Nau III when I was superintendent of the only U.S. Mexican War property in the National Park System while he served as Chairman of the Texas Historical Commission. John's passion for Civil War and American history would soon become apparent to me as well as how much I would value his guidance and friendship. Whether in his business life or supporting causes to protect our nation's most special places and stories, John remains a very strong influence and mentor in my life, for which I am eternally grateful.

In addition to former directors of the National Park Service, I am also deeply grateful for the support and friendship of my former colleague P. Daniel (Dan) Smith, who came out of retirement to serve as deputy director, exercising the authority of the director of the National Park Service for twenty-one months in the Trump Administration (now retired).

When asked by the Secretary of the Interior on two separate occasions who should serve as the next director of the National Park Service, Dan did not hesitate with his response.

From my deputies, chiefs of staff, superintendents, office and staff assistants, administrative officers, park rangers, U.S. park police officers, and many more colleagues past and present, I cannot adequately put into words how much I greatly valued and appreciated your hard work and friendship. A very special thanks to all of my amazing office assistants who kept me focused and who helped to fulfill the duties of my office—Kelly Fox, Janice DeSordi, Deb

Frauson, Monette Graham, Erika Breeze, Rachel Wheelus, Anna Womack, Bonnie Jenschke, and Carol Gonzalez.

It would take many more pages to appropriately thank all of those family and friends who also guided and helped me along my journey through our national parks. In addition, special thanks to all of my Latino colleagues both past and present who inspired me and through their own actions, helped to give me the confidence to achieve my dreams and aspirations in the National Park Service. I sincerely hope that they all realize that I was the ultimate benefactor of their time and support.

My sincere thanks to our dear friends April Landale, Grand Teton Association Executive Director; C. Scott Shafer, Professor and Head of the Recreation, Park, and Tourism Sciences department, Texas A&M University; Doreen Wise; Mary and Randall Kaufmann; and Yvette Benavidez Garcia (author of *Tango Mike Mike, The Story of Master Sergeant Roy P. Benavidez*) for their technical and editorial review, comments, and support of *Hola Ranger, My Journey Through the National Parks*.

In closing, this publication captures my life experiences growing up in Southeast Texas and the people I met along my journey in protecting and managing our nation's most special places. Most importantly, it reflects and embodies my profound belief in faith, family, and country.

CONTENTS

FOREWORD

The letter was dated April 4, 1962, and addressed to Mr. Robert G. Stanton from Secretary of the Interior Stewart Udall. It went on to read, "This will confirm your selection for appointment as seasonal park ranger at Grand Teton National Park for the coming summer. The uniform you will be wearing is familiar to the millions of individuals who visit our national parks annually. I am sure that your work assignment in one of the great areas of scenic beauty in this country will be both pleasant and rewarding."

My journey through the national parks began in 1962 when I borrowed $250 to buy a uniform and a train ticket to Grand Teton National Park in Moose, Wyoming. As a seasonal park ranger during the summers of 1962 and 1963, I experienced my first visit to a national park. It was quite the experience as I had never been outside of my home state of Texas. In 1997, and after thirty-one years of service with the National Park Service, I would become the first African American to administer the agency.

Hola Ranger reflects upon many of the same experiences that I had encountered growing up in Texas as a person of color, everything from travels outside of our home community and comfort zone, to having the privilege and honor of wearing the "green and gray" uniform of the National Park Service. It also provides a first-hand view of David's journey through the national parks, the people that influenced him, and his life experiences along the way.

As with me, and having sat in the director's chair, David had a front row seat to what it was like to lead the National Park Service while managing COVID at 419 park units, demonstrations involving racial and social unrest, and much more.

He also provides the reader with a potential blueprint designed to help ensure that all Americans are included in the national narrative while building the next generation of conservation stewards, leaders, and advocates. In addition,

Robert G. Stanton, seasonal park ranger
Grand Teton National Park, 1962
Stanton Family Photo

he reflects upon and honors all of the dedicated women and men of the National Park Service who protect our nation's most special places and all of their stories.

My dear friend, former Secretary of the Interior Stewart L. Udall (my former boss) once said, "As the National Park idea flowered in this century, it produced a special kind of conservationist—the park ranger—who has made unique contributions to our understanding of the natural world and its relationship to our future well-being."

Like me, I know you will enjoy *Hola Ranger, My Journey Through the National Parks* by my dear friend, fellow Texan, and fellow ranger, David Vela.

Robert G. Stanton
15th Director of the National Park Service

INTRODUCTION

Growing up in Connecticut provided a number of opportunities to enjoy nature and to recreate within some of the most beautiful areas in the country. These experiences helped to create a foundation for a career and livelihood in the parks.

My love for parks, and working with those who serve and protect them, was realized when I served for twelve years as the Director of Florida's State Parks, which was recognized as the best state park system in the country. I was nominated by President George W. Bush, confirmed by the U.S. Senate in 2001, and became the sixteenth Director of the National Park Service. In doing so, I became the first woman in the agency's history to hold that position.

During my tenure as Director, I had the opportunity to meet David Vela while he served as the Texas state coordinator for the National Park Service in 2003. It was at that time that I had the opportunity to get to know David and his passion for the National Park Service. During one particular business trip together, David would endure an experience that would remind him of that trip for the rest of his life. You will have the opportunity to read about that later.

Over the course of his thirty-eight years of public service, David provided many hundreds of speeches in venues ranging from classrooms to large conference settings. On many occasions, he was encouraged to put his stories and life experiences in writing. Heeding that advice, and over eight years in the making, he produced *Hola Ranger.*

David devoted his entire career in public service to taking on causes greater than himself. In addition, he effectively engaged others and led by example in achieving diversity, relevancy, and inclusion both in the workforce and workplace throughout his entire career in the National Park Service. What he learned along his journey about his Latino heritage is equally compelling.

Hola Ranger, My Journey Through the National Parks not only puts the reader in the car as he makes his journey but also provides a roadmap for future generations of conservation stewards and advocates, especially communities of color.

Taking us from his humble beginnings in the farmlands of Southeast Texas to meeting and working with U.S. Presidents and First Ladies, this is a must read. In addition to chronicling

his life experiences, *Hola Ranger* will help to inspire the next generation of diverse public servants as well as all who are interested in pursuing causes greater than themselves.

Fran P. Mainella
16th Director of the
National Park Service

CHAPTER 1

GEORGE

Throughout the over-one-hundred-year history of the National Park Service (NPS), a number of individuals stand out as champions and leaders in helping to achieve the mission, and whose actions have stood the test of time.

As we sat listening intently to Dayton Duncan introduce clips of the Ken Burns upcoming PBS series *The National Parks: America's Best Idea* during a National Park Service Superintendent Summit in 2008, we were about to learn about one of these champions, an American biologist.

As a recently appointed regional director, I was sitting next to a couple of Latino superintendent colleagues watching the story of George Wright unfold before our very eyes. At the conclusion of the brief clip, we all looked at each other in total amazement that we did not know this legendary NPS biologist was a Latino!

With many decades of NPS service between us, we were in awe and embarrassed. We had each known of the society that bears his name, The George Wright Society, and of his achievements, but had never heard of his middle name "Melendez."

Motivated by the actions of the park to control predators and encourage the public not to feed bears and other animals, George decided to conduct a four-year wildlife survey in 1929 that he funded himself for the national parks. At that time, the National Park Service did not have a program or full-time staff to perform field research to further wildlife conservation interests.

The *Fauna of the National Parks of the United States, a Preliminary Survey of Faunal Relations in National Parks,* was published in 1932. The report provided preliminary findings and recommendations on the survey.

George was designated as a member of a "Commission to represent the United States in conferences with a Mexican Commission to formulate policies and plans for the establishment and development of international parks, forest reserves and wildlife refuges along the international boundary between Mexico and the United States ..." in 1936.

Upon leaving Big Bend National Park (Texas), and traveling near Deming, New Mexico, an on-coming car blew a tire and impacted the car that George was driving head-on. He and an NPS colleague Roger Toll were both killed in the accident. George was only 31.

George's work continues to inspire and influence the NPS and resource managers today—including me. While at a George Wright Society conference in Portland, Oregon, in 2009, I had the opportunity to meet a family member of George, and made a pledge that I would share his story to help inform and inspire future generations of conservation stewards and advocates (to include Latinos).

The society that bears his name provides both cultural and natural resource managers with an opportunity to gather, share scientific and research developments, and celebrate his visionary ideals for public land management agencies. Upon learning of George, I became inspired and began to ask myself—what other Latino colleagues before or after George did I not know about? What were their stories, what did we have in common, and what inspiration could I draw from their work?

As for me, George was more than a visionary scientist; he is an inspiration for current and future generations of National Park Service employees, and Latinos as well. Sitting in that conference room with my colleagues, I began to reflect upon my own experiences and journey through the national parks.

CHAPTER 2

A COUNTRY BOY

It all began in rural Southeast Texas where a Latino country boy would one day rise to the highest position in the National Park Service as well as experience a world of opportunities and people along the way.

The history of my hometown of Wharton, Texas, was quite unique as the Republic of Texas had established the Caney Run mail route through the area in 1838. The town was named after two brothers, both leaders for Texas independence: John and William Wharton.

Growing up in the 1960s and 1970s in Wharton provided us with an opportunity to experience and build life skills that would serve me and my family well into adulthood. However, there were also times when we would experience the sting of discrimination and racism.

My mother would tell me stories of how in the 1950s they had to use the "colored" restrooms in the basement of the Wharton County Courthouse, which was located in the town square. Her mother and brother were able to eat in the local restaurants as their skin tone was light in color

but my mother and other relatives had to eat in the kitchen or in the back of the establishment.

Raymond and Mercedes Vela, Author's parents, 2014, Vela Family Photo

At an early age, I would soon have my own encounters with racism in one of my first jobs as a teenager while performing odd jobs for an elderly gentleman who was Anglo. He would have me paint structures and do landscape work around his property. However, as he provided instructions for the day, he would also remind me that he needed to monitor my work as he did not trust "Mexicans." Needless to say, my days were numbered on that job, but that experience would last a lifetime.

I did not have to look far for my role models as they were just around the corner from my bedroom. My father (now deceased) worked the graveyard (night) shift at a sulfur company while attending classes during the day at the University of Houston, and my mother worked in administrative positions at our local junior college. Going to Sunday mass was an important family tradition, and my brother Michael and I served as altar-boys.

My paternal grandfather was a farmer and sharecropper, and even though he worked at the same sulfur company (for thirty-seven years) as my dad, his love of farming and working the land never left him. I would later discover through genealogy how instrumental farming and the love of the land was in the Vela Family history and DNA. My grandfather would always remind me of the responsibilities I had as his oldest grandchild, which continues to serve me well today.

My paternal grandparents had very little formal education. I remember as a small child visiting my grandparent's house, and my grandmother would ask me to get some meat from the freezer. To my surprise, the white butcher paper had different images of animals, which my grandmother had drawn, to identify the type of meat that she had purchased as she had difficulty reading and writing.

My maternal grandmother worked in a family-owned grocery store for the vast majority of her life and was well known and respected for her business skills and offering a helping hand to those less fortunate. Although small in stature, you knew she was someone who would not be disrespected.

(L/R back row) Author's father, Uncle Paul, Aunt Mary, and Uncle Ruben; (L/R first row) Grandma Victoria and Grandpa Epolito (Polo) Vela, 1970s, Vela Family Photo

All of my grandparents found a way to improvise and to navigate daily life, which was passed on to their children and grandchildren. Although we were not a family of financial means, family was and is everything, and we did not miss out on life's many offerings either.

The Vela Family Grandchildren, 1970s
(L/R first row) Andrew Vela, Peter Padia, Eric Vela, Bianca Vela,
and Susan Padia; (L/R second row) Michael Vela, Eddie Vela,
Steve Padia, Judy Vela, and Lisa Vela; (L/R back row) Author,
Rick Padia, Grandma Victoria, and Grandpa Polo, Vela Family Photo

Surf fishing with my Uncle Sonny at Matagorda Bay catching red fish and huge drum while snacking on salami and cheese on top of saltine crackers was the life! In addition, we went boating on the river which feeds Matagorda Bay for flounder and sand trout with my father-in law Domingo and brother-in law Eliseo. Matagorda Bay and the surrounding shorelines provide critical habitat for nesting birds, shrimp, and blue crabs.

We also engaged in other outdoor activities that included everything from picking pecans in local cow pastures and collecting Coke bottles to pay for trips to the movies, to the joys of playing baseball and football with family and friends. Some of my favorite family memories involved food, whether eating tacos on the road, my grandpa's famous barbecue, or an ice-cold watermelon on a hot summer day.

We lived less than sixty miles from the big city of Houston, and would travel to the city to see Houston Astros baseball games or go shopping during the holiday season. It was our practice when traveling to Houston to pull out the tacos right after passing the landmark Tee Pee Motel. Built in the 1940s and restored and re-opened in 2006, it is a classic motel, with rooms inside Indian teepee-shaped buildings. We only traveled less than five miles from our home but it was taco time!

Playing sports, especially baseball and football, was a Vela Family tradition. My dad decided to serve as a Little League baseball coach, and taught my brother and I the fundamentals of baseball. As we moved through the different leagues, I would make the All-Star team and proudly wear the team uniform with our town name "Wharton" emblazoned on the front of the jersey. I would later have the same sensation and feeling of pride as I put on our high school varsity football jersey many years later.

Playing football with my Uncle Ruben, brother Michael, and the Padias (our cousins Rick, Steve, Peter and on occasions Susan) as well as with our fellow Latino kids in the neighborhood were truly fun and lasting memories. Like college bowl games, our pick-up football games were fondly known as the

"Chili Bowl." One of the standouts of these pick-up games was Victor (Vic) Erevia, who would later serve as my future wife's 15th birthday or "Quinceanera" escort.

After having completed a tour in the U.S. Navy (during the Bay of Pigs era), my dad would later teach judo to his children and Latino kids in the neighborhood to include Vic. While in junior and high school, Vic was a stellar football and baseball athlete and would later play collegiate baseball. He was our varsity football quarterback and played with great tenacity. Heaven help you if you missed your blocking assignment on the offensive line when you came back to the huddle as you would rather endure the wrath of the head coach than Vic!

Upon graduating from college, Vic's dream was to work for the United States Secret Service. He soon realized his dream and became a special agent. Due to his hard work and dedication, Vic rose through the ranks to become a senior

executive and the first Latino special agent-in-charge of the United States Secret Service Presidential Protective Division for President Barack Obama.

Special agent-in-charge, U.S. Secret Service, Victor Erevia (in background) with President and Mrs. Obama, Erevia Family Photo

Vic and I would later work in our nation's capital at the same time – two Latino senior executives working for our federal government from Wharton, Texas – both serving and protecting. Upon leaving his post in the White House, Vic was named Assistant Director for training in 2014, and upon his retirement, became a senior executive in employee security for a major engineering and construction firm.

Victor and wife Lenora Erevia,
Erevia Family Photo

We are so very proud of Vic and his years of service in the United States Secret Service. In addition, his wife Lenora and their children remain very valued and important members of the Vela Family.

The author's family
(L/R first row) author's wife Melissa, mother, father, and author
(L/R second row) brother-in law Chris, author's sister Judy,
sister-in-law Gloria, and author's brother Michael, 2014,
Vela Family Photo

CHAPTER THREE

WHERE ARE WE GOING?

Like many households in Wharton, we had our black and white television set until we were able to afford the Zenith color television. One of my favorite television shows was Flipper, which was produced in the 1960s. It was the story of a game warden taking care of his two young sons along with a dolphin in Florida. More on Flipper later!

One summer during the late 1960s or early 70s, my parents decided to take the family to Yellowstone National Park. Why? Good question. We had no experiences, references, or reason to go to a national park other than it was a destination that American families needed to experience. So, with few financial resources and little trip planning, we made the journey of a lifetime.

As we made our way to Yellowstone with three young kids, we experienced many new wonders outside of our car window, and soon realized that we were not in Texas anymore. There were mountains, streams by the roadway, animals that were unfamiliar to us and smorgasbords (restaurant buffets). Mom realized that she needed to stay close to me, the oldest, as I would load up on the proteins, totally neglecting the green stuff.

During one of our grocery stops along the way, we needed to buy some ham for sandwiches to save costs in eating at restaurants. However, as my dad came back to the car, all he had was a bag of corn chips and bread. His explanation to my mom was that the ham was too expensive! Needless to say, we were not happy campers, but corn chip sandwiches soon became a Vela Family tradition.

To this very day, my mom has difficulty eating corn chips! As for me, when I open a bag, I think of that trip to Yellowstone. As we would pull into a hotel after a long day of traveling, we would unpack and immediately hit the pool. One of the things that we began to notice on our trip was that there were not a lot people who looked like us. Was it possible that Chicanos (which is what we were called back then) did not make trips to national parks? If so, why?

Prior to arriving in Yellowstone, we discovered the majestic mountains of Grand Teton National Park—oh my! There was no way to know at that time that this vision and experience would forever change my life.

When we finally arrived at one of the entrance stations to Yellowstone National Park, there was a ranger (performing fee collection duties) wearing a funny looking "Smokey the Bear" hat with a green and gray uniform and gold badge. Wow, this was a truly foreign, intimidating, and amazing place with geysers, wildlife, and a landscape that you would not find in Texas!

The wonders did not cease when we pulled up to Old Faithful. I saw a ranger (in a law enforcement capacity) wearing the green and gray uniform with a revolver strapped to his hip and preparing horses for patrol duties. I remember thinking what a job and place to earn a living! Well, this young Latino country boy was truly impressed and was going to learn more about the world of a national park ranger.

In addition to its administrative role in the early parks such as Yellowstone and Yosemite, the U.S. Army helped to protect forests and discourage robbers and poachers. Easily recognized by their uniform, the cavalry also wore the "campaign hat" now popularly known as the "Smokey the Bear" hat. However, for present-day park rangers, it is affectionally known as the "Flat Hat."

Although we were in a totally unfamiliar environment, for some reason we felt safe. Not having park visitors and employees who looked like us added to some initial discomfort and anxiety. However, there was something truly magical about this place. Even at a very young age, I somehow valued and appreciated that this place was truly a divine gift to humankind, and one that needed to be protected at all costs.

Our journey to Yellowstone and Grand Teton would eventually come to an end, although my exploration about the world of the national park ranger was just beginning. What did you have to do to wear that green and gray uniform? Did you need a college degree? What about job experience? Most importantly, could a Latino country boy from Wharton, Texas, ever work in a national park? I had to find out!

CHAPTER FOUR

PRETZELS AND APPLE CIDER

Well, it was soon time to pack the bread and the corn chips again for we were back on the road, this time to Ann Arbor, Michigan. My dad had obtained his Bachelor of Arts degree and was now pursuing a Master of Science in Social Work from the University of Michigan.

I have many fond memories of the two years in the early 1970s that we spent growing up as teenagers on the University of Michigan campus. We lived in married student housing, which was an extremely diverse community, though the middle school that my brother Michael and I attended was not that way. There were just a handful of Chicanos, and we were somewhat of a novelty. However, this proved to be an enriching experience.

There was much to do and experience within the married student housing community. Attending Wolverine football games, climbing and picking apples from the trees on the housing property, potluck dinners with our family friends the De La Islas—these were valued memories. As our family income was limited, I earned a couple of extra dollars for our family cleaning garbage dumpsters in our housing unit. I will never forget during cold days while attending Michigan football games the smell of hot apple cider and the taste of soft pretzels.

Having to walk to school in bone chilling weather as well as digging out our car in the parking lot from the snow were quite the experiences as well for a family raised in Southeast Texas. But I must admit, an experience with my mom at the local grocery store one day would serve as one of the most humbling and enriching experiences of my life.

We were waiting in line to check out when mom pulled out a booklet of food stamps. There was little doubt that we were poor, although it never felt that way. Mom had never mentioned it to my brother, sister, or me, but then why should she? We always had food on the table. But come to think of it, we sure were eating a lot of peanut butter and cheese dishes. This was the staple of the government food program, and we learned to make the best of it. I can give you at least ten different ways to eat government cheese!

I will never forget mom's explanation for why we were on food stamps: "We have always paid our taxes, and this was going to be a short-term experience until dad graduated with his master's degree."

Mom was true to her words. Pitching in to help make ends meet proved an invaluable experience on a variety of fronts as it brought us even closer together as a family, kept us humble, and taught us the value of being thankful for our blessings.

Later in life, I would come to know more about the President whose actions helped to provide my family with this helping hand. The 1970s was an active time for the united farmworkers movement around the country. Chicanos would boycott and picket grocery stores because grapes were being sold at the cost of very difficult working conditions for farmworkers.

As teenagers, we joined the picket lines during the weekends and learned firsthand about the struggles of our brothers and sisters in the fields. While a tremendous learning experience, it was also an opportunity to expand our menu options, which included tacos and pot luck meals!

Taking advantage of the brief time we had in Michigan, my parents truly wanted this to be a learning experience. One day, they took us to a rally near Detroit to hear César Chávez, the founder of the national farmworker movement. I recall seeing a man small in stature but who spoke with moving passion about the plight of my Latino community. It was here, and from César, that I first learned about the importance of the land and of sustaining it. César spoke passionately about how blessed we were to be able to work the land and produce a product valued by society but also how this very land was poisoning our people due to pesticide use.

Our two years in Michigan provided a world of exploration and learning, everything from making new friends to expanding our life experiences. Dad obtained his master's degree, and before we knew it, we were heading back to Texas. Pass the bread and corn chips again, please—road trip!

CHAPTER FIVE

THE BEST CHEESEBURGER

As we settled back home into familiar surroundings in Wharton, we began our daily lives reconnecting with family and friends. However, one day, I decided to visit a hamburger restaurant owned by some family friends in the town square.

Upon walking into the restaurant, I noticed a long-time classmate behind the counter. In fact, we had gone to kindergarten together up to the seventh grade. Although Mirella Melissa Montelongo will recount the story differently, when I walked into the restaurant, she dropped the cheeseburger that she had been meticulously preparing!

Although this is my memory, I may be using some artistic license here. What I do recall for sure was seeing a beautiful and familiar face. Melissa went through school taking advanced and honor classes, and although we attended the same schools, we did not take the same classes. She was involved in band, student council, and extracurricular classes that were beyond my league and capacity.

However, on this particular day, we had some small talk about where I had been over the past two years and how

Melissa Montelongo, Senior,
Wharton High School, 1978,
Vela Family Photo

Author, Senior,
Wharton High School,
1978, Vela Family Photo

things were going. I must admit that when we had finished our conversation, I was very interested in spending more time with Melissa—little did I know then that it would be over forty years in the making as husband and wife. By the way, it was one of the best cheeseburgers I had ever eaten!

I attended Wharton High School during my sophomore year and had a relatively normal experience that included playing varsity football, singing in

Author and Melissa,
Wharton High School,
1978, Vela Family Photo

the school choir, and participating in drama productions. Melissa and I began to see each other on a more frequent basis and became an item. We stayed that way post high school graduation as well.

I had an interesting experience while playing a rival team during a varsity high school football game. While playing on the offensive line with my cousin Rick Padia, who was a wide-receiver and went on to play collegiate football, we were going after this brawny and tough middle linebacker the entire game. Each of us were getting in our shots at each other while "trash talking" in the process.

It was customary after the end of a game for us to greet our parents on the sidelines before boarding the bus to head back to our school. After this particular game, I saw the linebacker who my cousin and I were beating up on the entire game walking toward the sidelines where my parents were waiting.

I also noticed that my parents were talking to another couple, and this rival player was now talking with my parents. When I walked up to my parents, they introduced me to the linebacker—he was my cousin! I had no clue. So, one cousin was helping me to beat up on another cousin. Oh, the Friday night lights of Texas football.

Due to his work schedule, my Dad would miss some of my football games. However, I will never forget the times when he would stay up to fix me a late dinner after the game to talk about how things went as well as school life—and if I had any homework. Those were truly special memories.

In the course of my school work as well as in recalling that the national park rangers I had seen in Yellowstone had to do public speaking, I realized that I did not have these skills or abilities. I also had no desire and or interest in public speaking until I started taking both drama and speech classes in high school.

In addition to learning the art of public speaking, I knew that I had to gain some type of experience in the field in order to make myself marketable for a park ranger position. In doing so, I discovered the United States Youth Conservation Corps (YCC).

The YCC is a summer youth employment program that engages young people in meaningful work experiences in national parks, forests, wildlife refuges, and fish hatcheries while developing an ethic of environmental stewardship and civic responsibility. YCC programs are generally eight to ten weeks, and members are paid the minimum wage for a forty-hour work week.

Author (L/R, second row from top, second enrollee),
Anahuac National Wildlife Refuge, YCC program, 1976,
Vela Family Photo

In the summer of 1976, I was a YCC enrollee at Anahuac National Wildlife Refuge, which is part of the U.S. Fish and Wildlife Service National Wildlife Refuge System near Houston in Anahuac, Texas. Established in 1963, the 37,000-acre refuge cuts through ancient flood plains, creating vast coastal marsh and prairie boarding Galveston Bay in Southeast Texas and serves as home to migratory birds, alligators, and other wildlife.

As a co-ed camp, we lived in an old school house and performed a variety of duties at the refuge from trail construction to habitat restoration. I was elected by my peers to serve as the male representative of our camp and was responsible for discipline and camp assignments. It was also my first experience with alligators and in not seeing Melissa for weeks at a time. I could not wait for mail call and to receive her letters as this was also my first experience away from the comforts of home.

I thoroughly enjoyed my YCC experience and applied for another summer season in 1977 with the U.S. Forest Service. An all-male residential camp, I was making a whopping $2.60 per hour. The Caddo National Grasslands are located near Bonham, Texas, and provide grazing land for cattle and habitat for wildlife in addition to a variety of recreational opportunities.

We performed a number of conservation projects from trail construction and rehabilitation to removing old barbed wire fence lines. As a youth leader, I was in charge of a group council and helped to develop leisure activities after work hours. I will never forget the experience that I had during a break after a hot day of removing fencing.

One of my colleagues decided to chase an armadillo through some brush but did not see the hidden barbed wire. We soon heard the cries of pain and for help as we reached his location and found that he had sliced his stomach open on the barbed wire fencing.

I joined a couple of my colleagues and a supervisor who drove us and our injured colleague in a school bus that we used for transportation to the nearest medical facility, which was some distance from our camp. My colleagues and I took turns putting pressure on his exposed wound while trying to keep him from going unconscious. We were successful,

R/L, author with YCC Enrollees and Forest Ranger first from right, Caddo National Grasslands, 1977, Vela Family Photo

and after receiving many stiches, he was cleared to return to camp and to never chase armadillos again.

Participating in theater productions in high school gave me the confidence and skills in public speaking but also helped to pay my college tuition at Wharton County Junior College (WCJC) where I obtained a scholarship and an associate of arts degree in Theater. WCJC is well known nationally for their theater arts program.

One lasting memory I have was auditioning and winning the role of the Tin Man in the college's production of *The Wizard of Oz*. My suit was made out of a fiberglass compound that was designed and made by the college's art director.

Between the suit and silver face paint, I would endure serious migraine headaches after each performance, which had capacity crowds. What an experience!

During a sold-out matinee performance, I had an experience that after forty years of silence I am now making public.

Wharton County Junior College's Production of the Wizard of Oz, L/R, Author ("Tin Man"), Milton Hollis ("Cowardly Lion"), Abel Suaste ("Scarecrow"), and Amy Acosta ("Dorothy"), 1979, WCJC Photo

As the Tin Man, and before meeting Dorothy in this scene, I was to stand behind a tree. In addition, the Wicked Witch of the West swings on a rope from one part of the stage to the other. Well, prior to the performance, I felt that the tree was not in

Author, 1979, Vela Family Photo

the correct location and moved it just a short distance. You guessed it, the Wicked Witch hit the tree, left me exposed, and all that I could do was shrug my shoulders. Oops!

Of all of my experiences at Wharton County Junior College, there was one that would have a lasting and profound impact. While sitting in either a political science or economics class, an older but very engaging student was asking a lot of questions. He gave me the impression that he was no ordinary student. So, one day, I decided to ask him, "Who are you and what is your story?" I was not prepared for his answer, and little did I know then that I was talking to an American war hero.

CHAPTER SIX

AN AMERICAN WAR HERO

Born near Cuero, Texas, Roy P. Benavidez was the son of a Mexican father and a Yaqui Indian mother. But on May 2, 1968, while assigned to Detachment B56, 5th Special Forces Group (Airborne), 1st Special Forces, Republic of Vietnam, Master Sergeant (then Staff Sergeant) Roy P. Benavidez, United States Army, would become an American war hero.

Although his story now belongs to the ages, in 1980, he was my junior college classmate. Roy shared his life story with me and how he was trying to pursue the Medal of Honor so that his family could realize some of the benefits derived from our nation's highest military honor. So, upon introducing Roy to my father, who was administering a social services program housed at WCJC at the time, and as I was writing letters to the movie industry in order to bring national attention to his story, a lifelong friendship was created.

Roy and I spent many hours reminiscing on his life experiences, from fighting discrimination in his hometown to the tragic details of his service to the nation. On May 2, 1968, Roy's life would forever change. A twelve-man U.S. Special Forces patrol was surrounded on that day by a North Vietnamese

Army infantry battalion. Hearing a radio appeal for help, Roy boarded and later jumped from a helicopter in order to help his trapped comrades. In the process, he exposed himself to constant withering enemy fire, and despite enduring numerous severe wounds, Roy refused to stop and saved the lives of at least eight men.

When talking to Roy, it was difficult not to notice the scars that he wore in service to our country as his motto was always "duty, honor, country." Having been shot in the face, right leg, head, stomach, and thigh to include grenade fragments, it was difficult for him to sit down and or walk for long periods of time.

The time limit to receive the Medal of Honor had expired. Therefore, an appeal to Congress resulted in an exemption for Roy but the Army Decorations Board denied him the Medal of Honor. The board required an eyewitness account from someone who was present during the action. However, in 1980, Brian O'Connor, who was a radioman in the attacked Special Forces team, provided a ten-page report of the engagement.

Brian had been severely wounded and was evacuated to the United States before his superiors could fully debrief him. Brian had been living in the Fiji Islands and was in Australia when he read a newspaper account of Roy from his hometown newspaper in El Campo, Texas. When he learned that Roy was alive, Brian contacted Roy and submitted his report, which had confirmed the accounts that already had been provided by others.

While at my parents' home, I received a call from Roy. With exhilaration in his voice, he told me to pack our bags, we were going to Washington. Roy had been informed that he would receive the Congressional Medal of Honor! On a beautiful and clear day in our nation's capital on February 24, 1981, President Ronald Reagan presented Roy the Medal of Honor in the courtyard of the Pentagon where my dad, sister, and I joined members of Roy's family.

I will be forever grateful for this autographed picture from Roy stating, "To David Vela, Mi Hermano De Raza, A great American in every sense of the word. God bless those who help others. Thank you, David for all of your support. Best wishes, Roy P. Benavidez, Duty, Honor, Country."

Having heard in person the citation being read by President Reagan and reading it again now for *Hola Ranger* brings back a flood of emotions and memories of my dear friend. In addition, witnessing President Reagan place the Medal of Honor around his neck and watching in awe the military precision of the honor guards in the middle of the most powerful military complex in the world, was an experience I will not soon forget.

Master Sgt. Roy P. Benavidez with President Ronald Reagan, Medal of Honor Ceremony, Pentagon, Washington, DC, 1981 Vela Family Photo

*Author walking by the wall with his father (in front) on a tour of
past Medal of Honor recipients, Pentagon, Washington, DC, 1981
Vela Family Photo*

Following the event, we climbed a series of stairs to join
a receiving line, which consisted of President Reagan, Roy,
Mrs. Reagan, Vice President Bush, Mrs. Bush, and Roy's wife
Hilaria (Lala). When it was my turn, I stood in front of Roy,
and with the President by his side, we embraced wholeheartedly, and I recall him saying "We did it." It was very
hard for me to hold back the tears as I was now embracing
a decorated American war hero, although, I always believed
this to be the case even before he received our nation's highest
military honor.

We then proceeded to have lunch with selected guests at
the Pentagon. As we finished our meal, we were treated to a
guided tour of the Hall of Heroes where all of the Medal of
Honor recipients are recognized.

I recall seeing an individual wearing a brown suit with sandals among the group that was toward the end of the line and looked a little out of place—it was Brian O'Connor! I remember him asking me how I knew Roy, and I shared our experiences at WCJC.

He then told me how Roy saved his life, and how he was here today because of his actions. What a humble and unassuming man, and like Roy, I am eternally grateful for his correspondence to the Pentagon, and for his (and all of his military comrades before and after) who served our nation.

Following the tour, we had another meal in the secretary of defense's private dining room with our nation's highest military leaders and with Secretary Casper Weinberger. I have never seen so much "bling" at one time considering all of those in military uniform in the room to include what was on the china in front of us.

At the end of this amazing experience, we were asked by our military escort where we wanted to go in our nation's capital. My dad and I looked at each other, and I volunteered—the Department of the Interior. Prior to our trip, I had asked my good friend Lon Garrison from Texas A&M who I should visit at National Park Service Headquarters, and he responded Bob Nunn, a special assistant to the director.

Upon arriving at Mr. Nunn's office, I conveyed greetings from Lon and introduced myself and my dad and sister. Bob promptly asked what we were doing in town. I responded that we had just attended a Medal of Honor ceremony of a dear friend and had met the President of the United States at the Pentagon.

I had clearly gotten Bob's attention, and he asked what he could do for us. Without hesitation, I asked if we could meet the Director of the National Park Service, Russ Dickenson. He promptly picked up the phone to see if the Director was available and stated that there were some folks who just met the President and wanted to see him. I recall hearing a voice on the other line saying, "Send them on down."

As we were walking down the Director's corridor on the third floor of the Main Interior Building, I could not believe that I was about to see the Director of the National Park Service. By the time of this visit, I had entered the cooperative education program of the National Park Service at San Antonio Missions National Historical Park. While attending Texas A&M, I would work during the summer season gaining valuable work experience—more on this later.

So, in the course of one day, I was a witness to history in attending a Medal of Honor ceremony at the Pentagon, had a meal with the President of the United States, another meal with our nation's highest military leaders, and ended the day meeting the Director of the National Park Service. My only regret was that my wife, mother, and brother could not enjoy this experience with us as well.

Books were later written about Roy's life and military service, and we had the honor of having Roy baptize our son Anthony. Roy became very active in social causes and would stop by my parents' house for tacos on his way to see his fellow veterans at the Veteran's Hospital in Houston. Roy also loved to visit with school groups and would talk about the values that he believed in: faith, determination, and a positive attitude.

On November 29, 1998, at the age of sixty-three, my dear friend and former junior college classmate died. Roy would often say that he was proud to be an American, and even prouder to have had the privilege of wearing the green beret. When asked if he was a hero, Roy would respond that the real heroes are the ones who gave their lives to our country. His story and legacy now belong to the ages.

CHAPTER 7

AGGIELAND

Rising from the river bottoms near the Brazos River in College Station is Texas A&M University founded in 1876. Steeped in military traditions and homegrown values, it would wind up providing a sound educational foundation and a gateway to the National Park Service. The Department of Recreation, Parks, and Tourism Sciences (RPTS) at Texas A&M was and remains renowned for its field of study in tourism, park management, and interpretation (visitor services).

Upon taking a trip to visit Melissa, who had transferred from Wharton County Junior College to pursue a degree in accounting at Texas A&M, I was sold on the campus and all of the traditions and values it represented. So I decided to pursue a B.S. degree in Recreation, Parks, and Tourism Sciences at Texas A&M.

While pursuing my studies, I met one of the legends of the National Park Service, Lemuel (Lon) A. Garrison, who was a visiting professor at Texas A&M University. Lon spent over forty years in the National Park Service where he served as a superintendent at Hopewell Village, Big Bend, and Yellowstone. He also served as regional director of both the

Midwest and Pacific Northwest regions and was Director of the Albright Training Center in the Grand Canyon. Lon ended his career as a visiting professor at Texas A&M University and became a dear friend and mentor.

Lon encouraged me to apply for seasonal park ranger positions in the National Park Service. I did, and received a letter from De Soto National Memorial located in Bradenton, Florida, dated May 18, 1979 stating, "The major portion of your work will be at Camp Uzita where you will be wearing period costumes, cooking and eating period foods, firing sixteenth-century weapons, talking to Park visitors, and giving living history demonstrations." And the pay was $4.02 per hour!

On June 4, 1979, I signed my first Oath of Office, the first of many that would follow, stating, "I will support and defend the Constitution of the United States against all enemies, foreign and domestic ..." At nineteen years old, I was officially a seasonal employee of the National Park Service.

De Soto National Memorial was established in 1948 to commemorate the 1539 expedition of Spanish Conquistador

Hernando de Soto and his impact on the American Indian communities of the Southeast. One of the primary features of the park is Camp Uzita, which was constructed to resemble De Soto's base camp at the Indian village of Uzita.

Author as a seasonal employee at De Soto National Memorial, 1979, Vela Family Photo

During a holiday weekend, and having seriously missed my girlfriend of over five years, I decided to visit Melissa back in Texas. Little did she know how that visit would forever change our lives.

While taking her out to dinner at one of the restaurants in Wharton, I summoned my courage and on bended knee at the restaurant, asked if she would marry me. Unfortunately, I did not have a ring to put on her finger at that moment. Since it was a short visit, I was soon back on a plane to Bradenton, Florida. By the way, Melissa said yes, and we were married on May 24, 1980.

Melissa and I lived in married student housing and had many fond memories of our brief time at Texas A&M University (Aggieland). We warmly recall the many potluck dinners that we had with our neighbors as we were all in the same situation, working temporary jobs, attending class, as well as scrounging enough money to pay for Fighting Texas Aggie football games. This reminded me of our days at the University

The Married Couple,
May 24, 1980,
Vela Family Photo

of Michigan with my family in the early 1970s, which helped prepare me for my own collegiate experience.

Located within Austin's city limits, McKinney Falls State Park, a unit of the Texas Parks and Wildlife Department, provides visitors with the opportunity to follow trails winding through the Hill Country woods, explore the remains of an

Author, seasonal park ranger,
McKinney Falls State Park,
1980,
Vela Family Photo

Anthony Vela #29, Fullback,
Texas A&M University
Vela Family Photo

early Texas homestead, and enjoy Onion Creek as it flows over limestone ledges and into pools. Less than one month after our marriage, I was a seasonal park ranger at the state park, building upon my park experiences and work portfolio.

My primary duties involved the operation of the park's visitor center and to provide information to the visiting public on the natural and cultural resources of the park. In addition, I developed and presented formal evening talks at the park's amphitheater on park use, resources, and safety.

I would graduate from the University's RPTS Department as the "Silver Chaparral" recipient for my graduating class. The award stated, "Mr. Vela exhibits a rare blend of intellectual ability, maturation, energy and, above all, personal commitment which along with his demonstrated performance and devotion to professional preparation in his chosen field merit his selection as Outstanding Senior for fall, 1982."

Melissa graduated with a Bachelor of Business Administration degree in Accounting in August, 1982. Although we were always hopeful that our children would one day attend and experience Texas A&M, one of our greatest joys was realized when Christina and Anthony walked across the stage to receive their college diplomas in Aggieland. How ironic that they would both have classes with some of my former professors in the RPTS Department as well. My sister Judy would also graduate with a Bachelor of Business Administration degree in Accounting.

Christina Yvonne Kirkpatrick
Vela Family Photo

Christina received her Bachelor of Science Degree in Sport Management, and her diploma was presented by then Texas A&M University President Robert Gates, who would later serve as our nation's Secretary of Defense. Christina is now working in the field of education in Texas.

Seeing Anthony fulfill his dream of wearing the maroon and white of the Fighting Texas Aggie football team was a dream realized as well. He "walked on" to the team as a fullback and lettered three seasons. He received a full scholarship by then Head Football Coach Mike Sherman during his senior year as well as a Bachelor of Science Degree in Sport Management. Melissa and I made almost every football game that Anthony played, beginning with his sophomore year to include three bowl games.

No matter what sport and or collegiate level that one's son or daughter plays, it is a very proud moment when you see them put on the uniform of your alma mater! However, there was one experience that will remain with me for the rest of my life.

Prior to every home football game, player parents were allowed to see pre-game warm-ups near the field. There was a particular gate that I would enter while wearing all of my "player parent" paraphernalia. As soon as I arrived at the gate, I noticed what appeared to be security personnel wearing earpieces. My immediate thought was that it was the Governor of Texas but soon realized it was someone totally unexpected—a former President of the United States!

I was soon locking eyes with former President George H. W. Bush, who has his presidential library on the Texas A&M campus. While noticing all of my "player parent" regalia, the President quickly asked if I had someone playing on the football team, and I responded that my son was #29, Anthony Vela. Whereupon the President indicated that he knew Anthony, and that I must be very proud of him.

Wow, the President knew our son! I recall that I could not wait to see Anthony after the game to share my brief encounter with the President and to ask if he had met him. Anthony stated that the President would come to their practices and would make a point to meet and visit with each of the players. That explained it, and to this very day, I cannot remember who we played and or whether we won the game that day.

On December 5, 2018, Melissa and I would have the honor of joining United States Park Police and National Park Service personnel in saluting President Bush as his casket and hearse drove past the World War II Memorial in our nation's capital on his way back to Texas for the funeral. I will always be grateful for that brief moment in time with the forty-first President of the United States.

In addition to receiving my degree and the Silver Chaparral Award, my former department would honor me as the 2008 recipient of The Leslie M. Reid Alumni Award —"For Outstanding Professional Achievements, Integrity, Recognition Among Peers, and Genuine Concern and Support for the Department of Recreation, Park, and Tourism Sciences." For nearly forty years, what I learned and experienced within the RPTS Department and Texas A&M University continues to serve me well today. Gig 'em, Aggies!

CHAPTER 8

THE GREEN & GRAY

Four Spanish frontier missions, part of a colonization system that stretched across the Spanish Southwest in the seventeenth, eighteenth, and nineteenth centuries, are preserved as part of San Antonio Missions National Historical Park located in San Antonio, Texas.

Established on November 10, 1978, the park includes the missions of San José y San Miguel de Aguayo, Nuestra Señora de la Purísima Concepción, San Juan Capistrano, and San Francisco de la Espada. The park also includes a ranch, an aqueduct, and a series of archaeological sites. Mission Concepción is the oldest unrestored stone church in the nation, and the Espada aqueduct serves as the only functioning aqueduct from the Spanish colonial period in the United States. The park's first superintendent was José A. Cisneros.

The NPS operates San Antonio Missions National Historical Park in collaboration with the archdiocese and is responsible for all secular elements of the four missions, including buildings, landscape, and visitor centers. Cooperative agreements were signed on February 20, 1983.

In a letter dated May 20, 1981, from park superintendent Jose A. Cisneros, my journey toward becoming a permanent employee of the National Park Service began on these historic mission grounds while I was enrolled at Texas A&M. The letter stated, "This is to confirm your appointment as a Cooperative Education participant at San Antonio Missions National Historical Park effective June 1, 1981. You will be presented some unique opportunities in helping to establish this new park area. We believe that you will be an asset to the project and the Park Service in general. We look forward to working with you."

Upon successful completion of the program, it provided a pathway to permanent employment, and the fulfillment of a dream that began on a trip to Yellowstone National Park.

There were many enriching experiences and developmental assignments that I had while working in the cooperative education program at the park. One such experience was when I received museum curatorial training at Lyndon B. Johnson National Historical Park (LBJ) in December 1981.

To have a training opportunity at LBJ would have been a great experience in and of itself. However, to work with actual items and artifacts of a former President of the United States was phenomenal.

I received training by one of the legendary curatorial specialists in the National Park Service, Elizabeth (Libby) Hulett. Libby provided training on how to appropriately catalogue historic items according to NPS policies and standards. One of the items that I catalogued was a suit belonging to President Johnson that he wore at the White House. As I was holding his trousers, I remember saying to myself, "Wow, I am literally holding the seat of power!" Imagine being in a building containing national treasures, many of which the public would never see, let alone hold in their hands.

In a letter to my supervisor dated December 7, 1981, Libby stated, "He proved to be a quick learner and had a great interest in all aspects of curatorial training and work. I feel he should be commended for his interest. Besides his good learning ability he has a marvelous disposition and personality. He will be an asset to any park lucky enough to get him." Never in my wildest dreams would I have imagined that my days receiving training at LBJ in the early 1980s would set the stage for an even greater experience many years later.

We were the first permanent staff to operate the new national park unit in San Antonio and had to deal with separation of church and state issues. They were resolved in a legal opinion by the Department of Justice on December 2, 1982, allowing NPS management of the missions, while the archdiocese continued use of the missions as active churches.

I would become the first site supervisor of Mission San Juan, and had the honor of signing an operational agreement between the National Park Service and the Archdiocese of San Antonio.

Seeing national park rangers wearing the "green and gray" uniforms as well as the trademark "Smokey the Bear" hats was quite a sight within the four mission communities and the city of San Antonio. "Hola, Ranger" would soon be heard as we performed our jobs within the culturally rich and living mission communities, which we had the honor of preserving for current and future generations. For many living in these communities, we were mistaken for the U.S. Border Patrol, as our uniforms are very similar.

Author signing operational agreement, 1983, Vela Family Photo

Author with Russell E. Dickenson, 11th Director of the National Park Service, at an event at San Antonio Missions National Historical Park, 1983, Vela Family Photo

The National Park Service provides an array of training programs that included introductory, supervisory, and management courses, specific skills such as law enforcement, and senior-executive-level opportunities. One of the most memorable training programs that I attended was from April 10 to May 18, 1984.

The training program was entitled "Ranger Skills XV" and due to its popularity was a very difficult class to get into for relatively new employees of the NPS. The location clearly was an attraction, but it was what you were going to learn and experience while spending weeks in Grand Canyon National Park that was the real draw. Program participants would learn about the mission and core values of the NPS, how to do a grid search, group dynamics, and law enforcement ride-a-longs. They'd also hike the eight miles to Phantom Ranch at the bottom of the Canyon.

On top of that, the program was an opportunity to meet colleagues from different job disciplines from around the country who worked in small parks, large parks, and regional offices. Having an opportunity to visit and take a class photo with Director Dickenson was a real treat as well.

Truth be told, I am more of a front-country than back-country ranger but it was time to prepare for and then start out on the required hike! Traveling on remote trails while carrying a large backpack, sharing the trail with mules packing supplies to Phantom Ranch, and the prospect of sleeping in the Canyon were all uncharted territory for this ranger.

However, the majestic skies at night and the tremendous feeling of pride at now having a Canyon experience was a badge of honor for me—and all worth the sore knees and body aches that followed!

While a cooperative education student attending Texas A&M University and later as a permanent park employee, what I was learning and experiencing were not well reflected in my public-school history books. I was fascinated by what I was taking in about my Latino or "Tejano" heritage. Over three hundred years ago, the Spanish missions of San Antonio merged Spanish and native cultures, people, and lifestyles to create what South Texas families, including mine, embody today.

Author, prior to Grand Canyon National Park hike to Phantom Ranch, 1984, Vela Family Photo

First permanent staff at Mission San Juan—L/R Julie Canejo, author, and Lisa Garvin, San Antonio Missions National Historical Park, 1982, Vela Family Photo

CHAPTER 9

ROLLING HILLS

Pack the bread and corn chips, Melissa, we are heading to the rolling hills of Virginia! Upon remembering the iconic image of that law enforcement ranger at Yellowstone wearing his National Park Service uniform and revolver, I wanted to have that same experience. This would soon be realized at Appomattox Court House National Historical Park in Appomattox, Virginia.

Imagine walking the old country lanes where Robert E. Lee, Commanding General of the Army of Northern Virginia, surrendered his men to Ulysses Grant, General-in-Chief of all United States forces, on April 9, 1865.

The park encompasses approximately 1,800 acres of rolling hills in rural central Virginia and includes the McLean home (surrender site) and the village of Appomattox Court House, Virginia, the former county seat for Appomattox County.

In a memorandum dated September 14, 1984, from the park's superintendent, my lateral reassignment would be effective on October 14, 1984. It also stated "… the position requires the occupancy of government quarters located at the far end of the village. Because of its location and because the house is historic (it was here at the time of the surrender) we have developed guidelines for its occupancy."

We would soon be living in an original home (the Peers House), which was surrounded by a white picket fence with a cannon in the backyard. As a supervisory park ranger, I would be responsible for park law enforcement, interpretation, fee collection, and safety programs.

What I recalled from my previous studies was that the surrender occurred at Appomattox Court House. So, upon arriving at the park, I expected to see a table and two chairs in the courthouse. Wrong! I had a lot to learn.

The actual courthouse played no role in Lee's surrender as it was closed on April 9th due to it being Palm Sunday. The surrender took place in the parlor of the home owned by Wilmer McLean in the village of Appomattox Court House, Virginia. Wow, how could I have missed that when history was my favorite subject?

I recall our first night in the house and how dark it was living in the country, and I must admit that I was a little intimidated having just left the bright lights of San Antonio. As the park's sole law enforcement ranger, and living in the village in the Peers House, I responded at night to alarms and monitored the park's overlooks as well as other related interests.

Our daughter Christina, now ten months of age, would walk out on the porch to wave to all of the visitors taking pictures of the historic home. She is part of many rolls of film belonging to visitors who would photograph their park experiences.

The community of Appomattox was relatively small and rural at that time. I remember going to eat at a restaurant in town with Melissa and Christina and noticed an elderly person who kept staring at us. Well, she couldn't control herself, and as she was walking out of the restaurant with her companion, she asked, "You all aren't from here, are you?" I then replied, "No ma'am, we just moved from Texas." She then asked, "You look Hawaiian. What are you?" I answered, "We're of Mexican descent," and she replied, "Well, welcome."

Christina in the backyard of the George Peers House, 1984, Vela Family Photo

Since it was a community that had few Latinos at that time, I was prepared for that encounter to go a number of ways, but thankfully it was a harbinger of how we were treated in the community—with dignity and respect.

While learning about the developments in the parlor of the McLean House, I was fascinated by the story of Colonel Ely Parker. The formal copy of Grant's surrender terms was written by Colonel Ely Parker, a Seneca Indian. Upon seeing Parker, General Lee remarked, "I am glad to see one real American here." Parker later stated, "I shook his hand and said, we are all Americans."

As a person of color, I was fascinated by the role that Colonel Parker played in helping to end one of the most challenging and difficult periods in our nation's history. I then began to wonder, what role did my Latino ancestors play in the Civil War? Also, how many American Indians knew that one of their own was in the room, was a witness, and played a direct role in making history? I did not recall reading much about the role that people of color played in the Civil War during my school studies. However, twenty-eight years later, I would finally learn the fascinating truth.

The decision to move from one location to another can also be difficult for the nuclear family. I vividly recall having to explain our decision to move from San Antonio, Texas, to Appomattox, Virginia, to my in-laws. It was difficult for them to understand why we needed to move for my career in the National Park Service and why I was taking their youngest child out of Texas. It was not their fault, as I even questioned why we were going to Yellowstone on a family trip over a decade earlier.

Over the decades, my wife Melissa has played a very crucial and important role in our decisions to move from one park assignment to another. I have shared what I have learned and experienced with my colleagues, to include those of color, as they considered a move away from their nuclear families. In the case of Appomattox, it was to obtain law enforcement training and experience working in a Civil War park in addition to attending classes at the Federal Law Enforcement Training Center in Glynco, Georgia.

The scenario-based training was as real as you could experience, with practical exercises in simulated field settings such as campgrounds, trail heads, and traffic stops. Graduating in March 1985, this training would serve me well as I performed and managed law enforcement operations at the state and federal level later in my career.

Although the move did not involve a promotion but a lateral transfer at the same salary, it provided a world of exploration and experiences for my family and friends. Melissa

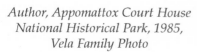

Police Training Class #9PT-503
Federal Law Enforcement Training Center
January 4, 1985 - March 7, 1985
Glynco, Georgia

Author (R/L second row, second from the left),
Federal Law Enforcement Training Center, 1985,
Vela Family Photo

found employment as a substitute teacher teaching keyboard and served as the high school varsity tennis coach.

In 1986, a new move pro-
vided an opportunity for a
promotion that sent Melissa,
Christina, and I further east
to the cobblestone streets of
historic Philadelphia and
Independence National
Historical Park.

Author, Appomattox Court House
National Historical Park, 1985,
Vela Family Photo

CHAPTER 10

CHEESESTEAKS

I applied and was selected to serve as a district ranger on May 28, 1986, at Independence National Historical Park. My primary duties were to oversee the Bishop White House, City Tavern, the park's visitor center, the First Bank of the United States, Thaddeus Kosciuszko National Memorial, and the Todd House.

Thaddeus Kosciuszko National Memorial preserves the home where wounded Polish freedom fighter Thaddeus Kosciuszko lived, and offers visitors a chance to learn about how this brilliant military engineer designed successful fortifications during the American Revolution.

On this assignment, I would walk along the very streets as our Founding Fathers, and I learned more about the history and places associated with the birth of our nation. On the way to my office each day, I would walk past Independence Hall and the Liberty Bell and would take in all of the sights and smells of this historic place. Of particular importance were the smells of grilling thinly cut steak—the famed Philly cheesesteak. Oh my, how I could not wait to make the short walk from my office to my favorite corner grill master for lunch.

During the opening of a Bicentennial exhibit in the Second Bank of the United States, I served as a liaison to the FBI. We were located in a building across the street that provided a good vantage point since a permit had been issued for a march in front of the Second Bank building. During the course of this assignment, I met a Latino FBI agent who shared information regarding the need for more Latino agents within the Bureau as well as within newly created organizations being formed within the federal government called inspector generals.

I have many fond memories of our time in Philadelphia. Among the modern-day intrusions, noises, and distractions, one could still find themselves within the Colonial and Revolutionary War period thanks to the preservation efforts and stewardship of the National Park Service and the citizens of Philadelphia.

Philadelphia provided a number of firsts for my family, such as eating our first bagel, cheesesteak, and cheesecake! We still enjoy these tasty treats although not as often, and in smaller portions.

Although I was thoroughly enjoying my job as a district ranger and my life in the National Park Service, the prospect of moving up the salary chart in order to support my family, which would soon add another member, had to be considered.

The description of the federal special agent position stated, "They serve in criminal investigations work with highly irregular hours on frequent occasions; and the work has a high-risk quality, involving threats of bodily harm and personal risk, depending upon the case assignment." I was now an agent working in New York City.

Working at 26th Federal Plaza, in the heart of Manhattan, was quite an experience, and was radically different from anything that I had done previously. For one thing, I would have to take an Amtrak train from Princeton Junction Station in New Jersey, the PATH train from Newark into the World Trade Center, and then walk the few blocks to my office each day.

While on the train to work, it was clear who was on board—the Wall Street crowd. It was truly something seeing these professionals dressed in their best business attire with hair and everything else neatly in place. However, at the end of the work day, you could also tell who had a good business day and who had not based on their mood and appearance.

As a special agent, my job was to investigate fraud, waste, and abuse within the programs of the United States Department of Health and Human Services. Our areas of focus were the states of New York and New Jersey as well as Puerto Rico. We also had an office in East Orange, New Jersey.

The vast majority of our investigations were in New Jersey and New York City and involved everything from the illegal counterfeiting of social security cards to fraud committed by medical suppliers and health care providers.

I was not used to the hustle and bustle of New York City. In addition to all of the tools that I was given to perform my job, to include the wearing of a trench coat in the winter months, my rosary was kept in close proximity!

Just getting to where I needed to go, whether to interview a witness or execute a search warrant, was an experience as you would either take the subway or an unmarked government vehicle. I recall one of our newest special agents having to take a course in order to obtain her driver's license as she grew up riding the subway her entire life.

This was also the late 1980s when the city was in a much different place crime-wise than the present day. Performing white collar criminal investigative duties on the streets of New York City with some of the most dedicated public servants around was a true honor and experience for this country boy from Texas. However, with my father-in-law experiencing serious health issues and with our newest addition to the family in tow—our son Anthony (born on February 27, 1988, in Trenton, New Jersey)—it was time to leave the east coast and head back to Texas.

Upon arriving back home in Wharton, I was not ready to leave the world of investigations and landed a job as a special enforcement operations investigator with the Child Support Enforcement Division of the Office of the Attorney General of Texas. Although my office was located in Houston, we performed criminal investigations related to delinquent child support orders throughout Texas.

While working for a state agency, I would meet a number of elected officials at every level of government while in the performance of my duties. There was one in particular who would help provide a very lasting and memorable experience.

CHAPTER 11

MICKEY

Renowned for his commitment to health, children, and the elderly, I had heard that congressman George Thomas "Mickey" Leland was looking for a special assistant for Hispanic affairs for his district office in Houston, Texas. I had also learned that there was going to be stiff competition for the job.

Although I never had any ambitions to pursue a career in the legislative branch of the federal government, Congressman Leland had an amazing reputation for taking care of his constituents, championing a number of social causes, and for getting things done.

I recognized that having the support of an associate or colleague of the congressman would be of tremendous benefit, and I was soon introduced by a close family friend to state representative Roman Martinez, whose legislative district was similar in scope to the 18th Congressional District.

As with the congressman, state representative Roman Martinez had a very strong and positive reputation among his constituents and was making a name for himself in the Texas Legislature. Upon being introduced and meeting the representative, he agreed to support my candidacy for the position, which culminated in a lifelong friendship.

I will never forget my interview with the congressman. It was on a Saturday in his district office in the federal building in Houston (which now bears his name). I was dressed in my Sunday best and knocked on his office door. I remember the congressman opening the door wearing a t-shirt, shorts, and sandals with his young son by his side. I said, "Congressman Leland, it is an honor to meet you, sir." He replied, "David, it's Mickey, and come on in." I was sold at that very moment and knew that I wanted this job!

We went to his office to begin the interview. After some small talk, Mickey stated, "I like what you have to offer. Now let's talk about what I want you to do." I got the job! We spent the next thirty minutes talking about what he planned for my position, which mainly involved assessing and helping to minimize the growing in-fighting among elected and appointed Latino leaders within his Congressional District, which was becoming increasingly Latino. I was now a congressional staffer.

While on a fact-finding mission to Ethiopia, Mickey's plane crashed in early August 1989. A total of fifteen people,

Author, Special Assistant, Houston District Office, 1989, Vela Family Photo

including Mickey, died in the crash. Whether it was feeding the most needy around the country and the world, or ensuring that we maximized the collective talents in our own neighborhoods, Mickey was a true servant of the people.

In the very short time that I worked for Mickey, I was inspired by how he used politics to serve a common good and causes greater than himself. In fact, it inspired me to run for local office on the Board of Trustees for the Wharton Independent School District. I would be running for an unexpired term with two opponents.

The challenge for me in running for office was that a previous Vela had run unsuccessfully in a school board election back in the 1970s—my father and role model. Although highly educated and actively involved in social causes within the community, it was apparently not the time for a Latino to hold a public office.

I recall members of my family reminding me of the stress and anxiety that we all felt with my dad's election returns, but they were also encouraging me in the process—especially my parents and Melissa.

My campaign strategy was simple, as I was advocating for discipline in the classrooms, developing programs to address at-risk students, providing teachers with competitive salaries and benefits, and providing students with the skills and resources needed to prepare them for the challenges of the 1990s.

I also wrote an editorial piece for our local hometown newspaper to parents and students stating, "As a community, we must continue to play an active role in the affairs of our educational system. The Greek philosopher Aristotle once said, 'All who have meditated on the art of governing mankind have been convinced that the fate of empires depends upon the education of their youth.'"

The election returns were in, and were posted on the door of the junior high school gym on May 5, 1990. This time, and while voicing many of the same themes and interests of my dad's campaign, we won by a total of twenty-five votes! Upon pulling into our driveway, Melissa was the first to run to all the assembled with the good news that we had won the election.

Word quickly reached those who were in the back yard— my grandfather, dad, and one of my uncles. We promptly embraced each other as it was truly an emotional moment. To this very day, I recall my grandfather (a former sharecropper with an elementary school education) stating that he never thought that this day would happen in his lifetime. Now, a member of his family had been elected to public office.

I was quick to share with my grandfather that he and my grandmother as well as their children (especially my parents) had opened the doors of opportunity for the next generation to walk through due to their faith, work ethic, and patience.

With Mickey now belonging to the ages, I would once again receive the support and assistance of my good friend, State Representative Martinez. As a legislative assistant, I worked in both his capital and Houston district office during a special legislative session as well as assisted with constituent matters. Meeting some of the state elected officials and becoming familiar with the Texas political process would serve me well in the years to come.

I became aware that the U.S. Equal Employment Opportunity Commission (EEOC) was hiring federal investigators within the Houston District Office. I applied, was selected, and was back in familiar territory conducting federal investigations. I learned a lot about our nation's civil rights laws and became proficient in investigating sexual harassment cases.

While working my caseload, I soon realized that there was a need to provide training and guidance in workforce diversity and related civil rights laws in both the private and public sectors. Seeing a strategic opportunity, a senior investigative colleague and I left the EEOC to form a consulting company.

I must admit, this was totally unfamiliar ground for me, as other than working odd jobs as a teenager, I had never worked in the private sector. We quickly began establishing our network of contacts and developed an instructional video. Making cold business calls as well as selling yourself to potential clients is indeed an art form and is not for everyone.

I greatly admire those who create, own, and manage their own businesses, but I soon realized that it was not for me. I was a public servant, whether at the state or federal level and missed the opportunity to serve others.

Although a truly valuable learning experience, I decided to pursue another opportunity to work for the Attorney General's Child Support Enforcement Office, this time as the Director of Field Operations in Austin, Texas.

CHAPTER 12

SERVING TEXAS CHILDREN

The year is 1991, and we had moved the family to Austin, Texas. In my new role, I was responsible for managing all of the investigative assets of the Texas Child Support Enforcement Office, which consisted of over seventy field offices throughout the State of Texas. Over the course of Attorney General Dan Morales's administration, there were a number of organizational changes that were made within his Child Support Program, and I held another position as director of client services.

There was one experience, however, in 1996 that caught me totally by surprise. I received a call to attend a meeting. Not knowing the nature of the meeting, I did not know how or what to prepare for. I was told that the attorney general had just removed the Texas child support director, and I was to be his successor. I also had to prepare remarks for me and the attorney general for an upcoming legislative committee hearing as well.

In 1988, I had started my career in state government as a special enforcement operations investigator with the Child Support Program, and nearly ten years later, I was serving as director. Still trying to process the rapid turn of events, I was ready to provide testimony before a House legislative committee. In his closing statements, the attorney general deviated from his prepared remarks by stating that when you are speaking to Director Vela, he is speaking on my behalf.

The attorney general then left the room with members of his leadership team and security detail, and it was show time. I recall walking up to the podium, pulling out my prepared remarks, and stating, "Mr. Chairman and members of the Committee, it is a pleasure..." That was as far as I got with my prepared remarks since I was interrupted by the committee chairman, who asked, "So what makes you think you are qualified to run the Texas Child Support Program, what role did your wife play in the attorney general's campaign, and do I understand correctly that you were a park ranger?" This was my introduction to the world of Texas politics in the state capital.

After what appeared to be hours before the committee, I was done. My first thought was, "What just happened, and what did I sign up for?" Then I became angry about my wife being brought into the hearing, as that made it personal.

Melissa was watching the proceedings on close circuit television in one of the attorney general's offices. As I left the state capital, I proceeded back to follow up with the attorney general. I will never forget what he said upon my arrival. The attorney general reminded me that he meant what he had said in his closing remarks, and that he left the hearing so that I could stand on my own.

I will always be grateful to the attorney general for the confidence and support that he provided to me during my two years as director, and for his friendship to me, Melissa, and our children.

I thoroughly enjoyed serving as the administrator of the Texas Child Support Program, which consisted of 2,500 employees located in over seventy field offices throughout Texas. Importantly, I got to work with all of our dedicated employees who worked to seize assets and establish and execute orders designed to provide for the needs of Texas children.

I had the honor of serving on a Criminal Child Support Enforcement Task Force created at the direction of the President of the United States. The task force was headed by U.S. Attorney General Janet Reno and was created to review and consider national strategies designed to achieve greater amounts of child support collections on behalf of our nation's children.

I was honored with a "Distinguished Service Award" from the Honorable David Gray Ross (commissioner, Federal Office of Child Support Enforcement) on January 27, 1998, "In Recognition of His Distinguished Contributions Toward Giving Hope and Support to America's Children." Following the award ceremony in Washington, DC, the state child support directors (and spouses) who were honored had a working lunch with a representative of the President's domestic policy staff at the White House.

In the Spring of 1998, all of the program chiefs were called into the attorney general's conference room and were informed by him that he was not seeking a third term. In the State of Texas, the attorney general is not appointed by the governor but is an elected statewide officeholder. His decision had a direct and personal impact on me and Melissa, as she was an assistant to the first assistant attorney general.

The attorney general had made it clear that he was going to ensure that we had jobs and asked each of us in private meetings for our thoughts regarding our employment interests.

When it was time for my meeting, and without any hesitation, I was ready to go back to where I began my career in public service. The attorney general asked me if there was someone that he could call on my behalf. There was: the Director of the National Park Service. Robert (Bob) G. Stanton was the first African American director, and the fifteenth director in the agency's history. Director Stanton was also the first director to be nominated by the President and confirmed by the United States Senate.

In his letter dated February 25, 1998, to Director Stanton, the attorney general stated, "During my two terms in office,

Author with Bob Stanton,
the first African American
director of the National
Park Service,
Vela Family Photo

Mr. Vela held various director-level positions within my Child Support Division. Approximately two years ago, I appointed him as my Child Support Director. While serving as director, our child support program now ranks second in the nation in paternity establishments and sixth in total collections. Many of our programs and operational initiatives have been declared 'models' and shared with our colleagues around the country."

Over a period of two years, we were successful in improving customer service, relations with the Texas legislature and local elected officials, as well as the amount of child support collected for Texas children. I will always be grateful to all of our program staff, state elected officials, county and local partners, courts, and law enforcement agencies within the State who worked together with us to make a difference.

History, and the people of Texas, will ultimately judge all of the efforts and actions of the forty-eighth attorney general of Texas. For me personally, I will always be grateful for his friendship and the opportunity to provide for the needs of the children of Texas.

CHAPTER 13

JOURNEY HOME

I became aware of a vacant superintendent position in Brownsville, Texas, which is the site of the only U.S. Mexican War property in the National Park System—Palo Alto Battlefield National Historic Site (now a National Historical Park). I include myself as one of the many who did not know much about the U.S.-Mexican War, let alone the first battle.

I applied for the position, and with the support of Intermountain Regional Director John Cook, we were back home in the National Park Service, this time as a park superintendent. On September 24, 1998, the news release read, "David Vela Returns to the National Park Service as Superintendent at Palo Alto Battlefield National Historic Site."

Prior to my arrival, the park had prepared operational documents and had purchased important battlefield tracts. However, it did not have any visitor facilities or personnel located at the battlefield. One of the first orders of business for this rookie superintendent was learning with help from the park's administrative officer, Oralia Fernandez, how to work the office fax and copy machine. It became very clear that I was going to need to perform these functions on my own.

On February 21, 1999, the headline of the *Brownsville Herald* read, "History's Time Keeper—Vela Has Big Plans, Hopes for Palo Alto." Written by reporter Tim Lopes, the article stated, "Today, most people who look around the site may see nothing but yucca, mesquite, and prickly pear cactus. David Vela, however, sees museums, a visitors' center, and miles of hiking trails filled with informational kiosks telling the story of the battle. He's the Palo Alto Battlefield site Superintendent."

As a first-time superintendent in the National Park Service, I learned a lot about park operations and building coalitions of support. With minimal operational and financial resources, we set upon a course to raise awareness within the community of the value of a fully functional and operational national park unit within their midst.

With the dedicated support of my staff, private citizens, elected officials, and community organizations, funds were raised and facilities were built on the battlefield. The vision that was reflected in the newspaper article on February 21, 1999, had now become a reality.

When reading the park's official web page today, visitors are informed of a visitor center that features an exhibit area with interactive exhibits, artifacts, Mexican-War-era military uniforms, and a fifteen-minute video, *War on the Rio Grande*, which provides an overview of the war. The visitor center also includes a small book store with over one-hundred book titles and specialty items. Visitors are encouraged to walk in the footsteps of history, where they will see a landscape very much like the one experienced by soldiers in 1846.

I had the pleasure of meeting an individual who remains a very important mentor and part of my life. John L. Nau,

*(L/R) Palo Alto Battlefield National Historic Site staff—
author, Oralia Fernandez, Aaron Mahr, Karen Weaver,
and Doug Murphy, 2000, NPS Photo*

III met with me to discuss Palmito Ranch, the site of the last
battle of the Civil War.

As President and CEO of the nation's largest distributor
of Anheuser-Busch products, John has a passion for service,
which is reflected in his involvement with community, civic,
and philanthropic organizations throughout the country.
John's lifelong interest and passion for American history has
served him and the nation well.

Words cannot adequately express how proud I was of
our entire park team and the community of Brownsville.
Failure at Palo Alto was not an option, and the facilities

John L. Nau, III,
Palo Alto Battlefield NHP,
Visitor Center Dedication,
2004, NPS Photo

John L. Nau, III (L) with Secretary of
the Interior Ryan Zinke (C), 2017,
Photo Courtesy of John L. Nau, III

today are a testament to the hard work of my staff, the value and importance of partnerships, and the efforts of succeeding park superintendents. They would take the vision articulated in the original park planning documents to even higher levels of achievement, and are to be commended for a job well done.

After spending four years as superintendent, I was asked by Intermountain Regional Director Karen Wade to serve as the Texas state coordinator for the National Park Service effective June 30, 2002. The press release dated June 7, 2002, stated, "In his role as Texas State Coordinator, Vela will serve as the primary representative to the Intermountain Regional Director, working closely with park superintendents within the State of Texas and coordinating National Park Service activities with congressional offices, state and federal agencies, county and city officials, and government associations."

In addition to my new responsibility, I also maintained line authority and oversight over the superintendent at Palo

Alto Battlefield National Historic Site. On January 24, 2004, I joined the park's superintendent, Myrna Palfrey, for the official ribbon-cutting ceremony of the new visitor center.

In my remarks, I stated, "With the flags of the United States and Mexico waving in the breeze, many of you joined me in a ceremony celebrating the opening of these hollowed grounds over four years ago. We dared to dream about one day opening visitor facilities in order to honor the memory of those who gave their lives over 150 years ago for a cause and country that they believed in. Today, that bold vision is now being realized."

Sixteen years after leaving Palo Alto, I would have the opportunity to approve my then administrative officer Oralia Fernandez as the superintendent for Palo Alto Battlefield National Historical Park. Oralia taught me many things as a rookie park superintendent, to include how to operate the copy and fax machine on my own!

The Intermountain Region of the National Park Service was divided into three clusters, and I was elected by my peers to serve a two-year term as chair of the Intermountain Region's Southwest Cluster, which consisted of thirty-nine NPS Units located in four states.

I was later asked by the Intermountain Regional Director Steve Martin to take on the role of superintendent

Author with Oralia Fernandez, superintendent, 2020, Vela Family Photo

of Lyndon B. Johnson National Historical Park in addition to my duties as Texas state coordinator.

In a news release, the regional director stated, "David brings a passion for parks and years of experience in building relationships and in enhancing partnerships with gateway communities, government agencies, and strategic partners. These qualities make him an excellent choice for the position."

So, on October 4, 2004, I began what was to be one of the most rewarding and enriching experiences of my career in the National Park Service. What an irony, as I would now be responsible for preserving and protecting those very same suits that President Johnson had worn in the White House that I had catalogued as a cooperative education student over 20 years previously. Now, I was the park's superintendent.

CHAPTER 14

A GRAND LADY

To this very day, all I can remember of my first meeting with Mrs. Lady Bird Johnson was thinking, *David, don't mess this up!* Our first meeting was in Luci Baines Johnson's conference room, younger daughter of President and Mrs. Johnson. Her Secret Service detail brought Mrs. Johnson in the room and seated her next to me.

I recall some "getting to know each other" conversation and my operational interests for the park as the new super-intendent. I just could not get over the fact that I was sitting next to a former First Lady of the United States and that I was now responsible for preserving and protecting the famed Texas White House and LBJ Ranch, to include the President's legacy for current and future generations to come.

I could not wait to get home to tell Melissa what this country boy had just done as part of my work day. On that drive home, it also dawned on me that I was one of the living legacies of the President's Great Society programs. From attending Head Start to benefiting from his food stamp program, I was now the superintendent of the national park bearing his name—what a true honor and blessing.

One of the first events that I attended was a "get to know the new superintendent" reception at park headquarters. It was a pleasure meeting and visiting with members of the local community as well as with some of our strategic partners. What made this event even more special was sharing it with Melissa and members of our respective families.

I recall taking my grandfather Polo Vela (the share-cropper) around the grounds of De Soto National Memorial when I was a seasonal employee in 1979. However, to have shared this particular moment with him and my parents as a superintendent was an emotional and memorable experience.

In Johnson City, park visitors can see how LBJ influenced his home town by bringing the resources of the U.S. government to bear on improving the lives of his friends and neighbors. On the LBJ Ranch, one can experience the serenity and beauty from which the former President drew his strength and comfort. It is also here that his final resting place is located.

Having the opportunity to work directly with the Johnsons' daughters Luci Baines Johnson and Lynda Robb as well as Lyndon Nugent (the President's grandson) was a memorable experience. I recall fondly driving in Lyndon's pickup truck around the LBJ Ranch discussing issues of mutual importance. Lyndon and I developed a very trusting relationship, and one that I greatly value and cherish to this day.

Working at park headquarters, which is located in Johnson City, Texas, was like working in a small community where time stood still. Not much had changed from when I received museum curatorial training at the LBJ Ranch in the early 1980s. The community had retained its small-town charm and character. One can only imagine what the town was like when President Johnson was a small child and later President.

As with all of my park assignments, I try to involve my family as much as possible in park events. At LBJ, it was enjoying the holiday season with Mrs. Johnson, Luci, her husband Ian, and their grandchildren as well attending events at the Texas White House.

During one particular event, our son Anthony was able to join me and Melissa. We were having lunch in the President's office in the Texas White House with Mrs. Johnson. Due to Secret Service restrictions, our ranger-driven ranch shuttles would drive up to the Texas White House, but visitors were not allowed to disembark from the vehicles.

Prior to serving as superintendent, I recall many times being on the shuttle wondering what was taking place in the House—was anybody watching us inside, and what was Mrs. Johnson doing?

While we were having lunch in the Texas White House, one of our shuttles was parked outside with park visitors. I recall Anthony whispering to me at our table, "Dad, I remember being on that shuttle many times, and now I am looking out at them from the President's office." Mrs. Johnson was sitting at a table next to us, and I recall telling Anthony, "This is a true blessing son, never forget this moment."

One of the challenges of serving as the park superintendent was to continue the planning protocols for the day when we would lose Mrs. Johnson to the ages. Previous superintendents had been involved with the family and the Intermountain Regional Office planning for this eventuality.

I must admit, I wanted to focus on the present, but also knew that we had to keep the plan current, fluid, and respectful of the family's interests.

The President and Mrs. Johnson donated the Texas White House, their private home, to the American people and to the National Park Service but retained lifetime rights to use the home. Following the death of Mrs. Johnson on July 11, 2007, the National Park Service began preparations to make the home available for public tours. The President's office was opened to the public on August 27, 2008, the one-hundredth anniversary of his birth. The living room and dining room were opened in June 2009. By December 2011, the entire first floor was opened to the public.

It would be extremely difficult for me to recount all of the amazing experiences that I had while serving as the park superintendent. I can recall being alone in the Texas White House from time to time assessing how best to preserve this national treasure for future generations. Also, I'll never forget the private dinners that Melissa and I had with Mrs. Johnson, Luci, and Ian in the home.

Imagine driving in the early evening hours to the LBJ Ranch on the main ranch road along the tranquil Pedernales River. You arrive at the white entrance gate and announce yourself to the Secret Service for entrance for dinner with Mrs. Johnson. At the Texas White House, you find Mrs. Johnson seated in a rocking chair outside of the President's office preparing to enjoy a Texas Hill Country sunset.

When you walk up to the porch outside of the President's Office, you are then greeted and enjoy the experience of a beautiful sunset with her while whitetail deer scamper around the grounds.

It is amazingly quiet and peaceful; then it hits you—if the rocking chairs and exterior walls of this historic house could talk, how many people—world leaders, national heroes, and ordinary citizens—who accomplished extraordinary things during the Johnson presidency had this same experience? On this night, it was a National Park Service superintendent and his wife, two Latino country kids from Wharton, Texas.

Photo provided to the author by Mrs. Claudia "Lady Bird" Johnson

I will never forget our last dinner together, and it would be the last time that I would see my dear friend as I had received a promotion to serve as the superintendent of the George Washington Memorial Parkway located in Washington, DC, Virginia, and Maryland.

I was given the autographed picture above of Mrs. Johnson, which has been proudly displayed in all of my offices to now include my residence. The picture states, "For David, With heartfelt appreciation for your dedication and caring stewardship of this place I love so much." As is fitting, her picture gazes upon me now as I write *Hola Ranger*.

The Johnsons' ongoing legacy of service in support of social, advocacy, and environmental causes continues with their daughters (Lynda and Luci), their husbands, children, and grandchildren. To this very day, Melissa and I value and enjoy their phone calls and Christmas cards as our love and friendship remains one of our most valued treasures.

What makes my time at LBJ so memorable is that it was personal and that it became an opportunity to return in kind what I had received. As a child, and later in life, my family and I benefited directly from many of the President's Great Society programs.

As the park's first Latino superintendent, my staff and I had the responsibility of telling the story of our thirty-sixth President and his (as well as Mrs. Johnson's) many lasting contributions to the nation.

One of the treasures that I have in my personal library is her publication *Lady Bird Johnson, A White House Diary*, which she gave to me. She inscribed "For David Vela— May your Park Service career bring you all the rich joy my own long acquaintance with the NPS brought to me in years past and still!—Lady Bird Johnson, Feb 8, 2001."

CHAPTER 15

MONUMENTS AND MEMORIALS

I had been asked by the first female and sixteenth Director of the National Park Service, Fran Mainella, to work a two-month detail in her office in Washington while I was serving as Texas state coordinator and prior to serving as superintendent of Lyndon B. Johnson National Historical Park. Director Mainella was interested in knowing why I was not applying for Senior Executive Service (SES) as well as GS-15 positions (highest federal career salary grade prior to SES).

I was extremely satisfied and thoroughly enjoying where I was in my NPS career and in working in the Texas Hill Country. Melissa and I had many amazing experiences at the LBJ Ranch to include one that is a stark reminder for me to this very day, especially when I get out of bed!

The story goes as follows. Director Mainella had a number of business commitments in Texas that included visiting Lyndon B. Johnson National Historical Park. My task for the day was to drive her from a residence in Austin to the LBJ Ranch on May 1, 2003. Of course, I was wearing my Sunday best suit with polished cowboy boots (no cowboy hat). Upon entering the residence, which had beautiful wooden floors, I offered to retrieve the director's luggage upstairs. Upon stepping on the first step, which was also wooden and polished, my two knees went into very different directions.

Upon letting out a little scream, I gained my composure and walked the remaining stairs to retrieve her luggage while all along the director was asking if I was OK. While walking down the stairs, and in great pain, I "rangered up" and drove the director to the ranch. Thankfully, Fran was on the phone the entire trip and did not notice the tears that were streaming down my face as I had injured my right knee, which was also the leg I was using to drive.

Upon concluding her business on the ranch, I drove the director to San Antonio for a meeting and then made the long trip home to Austin. By the time I had entered my driveway, my knee was swollen to the size of a baseball, and I needed help from Melissa to get out of the car. I had to have meniscus surgery on my right knee, and I think of my dear friend every time I get out of bed, and especially during cold winter months all of these many years later.

The thought of moving up the career ladder and working in the Washington, DC, area was appealing to me, and I

decided to apply for the vacant superintendent position at the George Washington Memorial Parkway. It was an extremely difficult decision since not only

Author with Fran Mainella, 16th Director of the National Park Service, San Antonio Missions National Historical Park, 2003, Vela Family Photo

would we be leaving a great park and community but family and friends as well. Time to pack the bread and corn chips as we were Virginia bound once again! However, this time, we had no kids in tow.

From having hundreds of thousands of visitors on the Virginia side of the Potomac River for the July 4th fireworks on the National Mall to an event in front of the Women in Military Service for America Memorial, (part of the entrance to Arlington National Cemetery), we had many memorable experiences over those two years that I served as superintendent.

It was a beautiful sunny day in our nation's capital, and I was seated on a stage facing down Memorial Avenue Bridge with the Lincoln Memorial in the foreground. Dr. Robert Gates had been the president of my alma mater, Texas A&M University, and was now serving as our nation's secretary of defense.

With a proud military tradition, it was customary to have fly-overs prior to Texas A&M football games by aircraft from our armed forces. As the helicopters flew over this particular event at Arlington National Cemetery, I leaned over to the secretary and whispered, "Kind of reminds me of Kyle Field." (Home of the Fighting Texas Aggie football team). He gestured with a big smile. We proudly display the graduation picture of our daughter Christina receiving her diploma from Texas A&M University with the former A&M president and defense secretary.

A series of unforgettable events would unfold when the park's deputy superintendent Jon James and chief ranger Vince Santucci came into my office for a meeting. A tip that was provided by a park neighbor during a ranger-led program led to an interview with a veteran. Additional information as well as recently declassified military documents and other research had revealed a super-secret interrogation center during World War II in an area known as Fort Hunt Park within the George Washington Memorial Parkway.

Oh my, we had information involving a super-secret interrogation center that was known only to those who were assigned to "P.O. Box 1142"! As a result of many hours of research and interviews by Chief Ranger Vince Santucci, the park's Cultural Resources Program Manager Matthew Virta, and Cultural Resource Specialist Brandon Bies, we learned of the systematic interrogation of Axis prisoners-of-war.

By the end of the war, Fort Hunt was used for interrogations of Germany's highest-ranking officers, top nuclear program scientists, and a limited number of high-ranking Japanese officials. The work of those involved in P.O. Box 1142 not only contributed to the Allied victory but also led to strategic advances in military intelligence and scientific technologies that directly influenced the Cold War and race to space.

Another visit by the chief ranger to my office would have a lasting and profound impact on my life. Towards the end of the workday on July 11, 2007, Chief Ranger Santucci asked if I had heard the news of the passing of Mrs. Lady Bird Johnson—I had not.

As you can imagine, a range of emotions had come over me. As I was processing the news of the passing of my dear friend, my office phone rang, and it was my friend and colleague Bill Line, who was our regional office's communications officer. Bill stated that the media wanted to interview me, knowing that I had worked with Mrs. Johnson.

As soon as I agreed to the interview, Bill put me on hold to answer additional media calls and requests for interviews. Well into the early evening hours, I gave multiple interviews on the banks of the Potomac River at Lady Bird Johnson Park.

Melissa had already flown to Texas to be with family, and I was scheduled to depart the following day. Having provided the interviews, I was still in the middle of an adrenalin rush and could not adequately process that Mrs. Johnson was no longer with us. Prior to her passing, Melissa and I had agreed, and were honored, to join family and friends at selected times to be with our close friend during her public viewing at the LBJ Presidential Library in Austin, Texas.

While standing next to her coffin, which was located at the top of the marble stairs, we would see individuals of all races and ages pay their respects to the former First Lady. Then, a lone Boy Scout dressed in his uniform climbed the stairs, paused, and gave a salute. It was at this very moment that I lost it; I mean my legs became weak, and the tears began to flow down my face—I had lost my dear friend.

CHAPTER 16

SIXTY-SIX

According to the position description, "The Regional Director exercises direction over mission-critical operations within the Southeast Region. Regional functions have impact on various issues that have national, regional, and/or local consequences."

Never in my wildest dreams would I have imagined overseeing sixty-six national park units let alone one as a park superintendent. Serving as a national park ranger was good enough for me, but ...

It all began with the encouragement of Director Fran Mainella to pursue opportunities in the Senior Executive Service, specifically the vacant regional director position for the Southeast Region of the National Park Service located in Atlanta, Georgia. Although I was a finalist, I was not selected. The director then asked that I consider serving in a 120-day detail assignment as an acting deputy regional director in the regional office, which I agreed to in 2003.

Never having worked in a regional office, I found myself lost and out of place in the beginning of my assignment. As a park superintendent, one can more easily determine needs and interests of park visitors as well as whether operational outcomes were being achieved simply by walking out of your office and directly engaging visitors and employees. This would prove more difficult managing region-wide portfolios as well as park units that were located throughout the southeastern United States and the Caribbean.

The detail assignment proved to be enlightening and challenging. While in Atlanta, I lived in a furnished apartment in the downtown area that was owned by Martin Luther King, Jr. National Historical Park. It was quite an experience walking to the bus stop in the historic district where Dr. King was raised and by his boyhood home.

Other than the downtown high-rise buildings that were visible from the historic district, one could imagine the young King playing in the streets and enjoying the safety and security of his neighborhood.

Having served as a park superintendent, and as Texas state coordinator, where I served the interests of national park superintendents with state legislatures and executive branch offices, proved handy in my acting capacity.

I could relate directly to the needs of my assigned parks and could address their interests in the regional office and on behalf of the regional director. However, I decided to end my detail assignment early in Atlanta and return to Texas.

I recalled as I was leaving the Southeast Regional Office for the last time that I would one day return as Regional Director if the opportunity presented itself, as I admired the great pride its workforce showed as well as the diversity of park units that comprised the Southeast Region.

Having been accepted into and completed the U.S. Department of the Interior's Senior Executive Service

Candidate Development Program in May 2006, I was now certified by the Department and the U.S. Office of Personnel Management and was ready to move further up the agency's corporate ladder.

With four years having passed since I left Atlanta, I would get a second chance. This time, and on May 11, 2008, the name plate on my desk would read "Regional Director" thanks to Mary Bomar, the seventeenth Director of the National Park Service. In announcing my selection, she stated "David came up through the ranks, beginning as a frontline park ranger," said Mary. "His early field experience prepared him to be a great superintendent and now he will apply those same skills as Regional Director."

With the dedicated support and commitment of over 3,000 employees, I would oversee parks from New Orleans, the Virgin Islands, and the Great Smoky Mountains. The experiences and memories that I had from this assignment over five years could fill this entire book.

In order to create a new environment and direction for the region, I sent an email message dated May 13, 2008, to all employees stating, "Prior to and upon my arrival, we will embark upon a course that will produce the following outcomes—treat each other, and all whom we come in contact with dignity and respect. We will hold all people and processes accountable, will meet deadlines, and will celebrate our successes. Safety will be incorporated in everything that we do, and is not an option. We will value and celebrate diversity—in our hirings, business practices, and civic engagement. We will make ourselves relevant to **all** visitors and communities."

What was exciting about this appointment was that I was also coming home to where my NPS journey began—the

Southeast Region—and De Soto National Memorial. This time, I would be overseeing De Soto National Memorial as Regional Director.

Despite some operational and leadership struggles over the years, the Southeast Region possessed some of the most dedicated and professional employees in the entire National Park Service. With their patience and support, we were able to collectively bring the pride back to the region—all credit going to my leadership and regional support team, my park superintendents, and employees.

The Southeast Region has a great diversity of park units, from civil war battlefields to national seashores. I recall a conversation with a colleague from our Washington headquarters office who wanted to get my perspective on how the promotional tagline "Civil War to civil rights" would play out within the Civil War units that I administered in the Southeast. The NPS was commemorating the Sesquicentennial (150th) of the Civil War; it was a good question, and I needed some help.

I quickly visited with my Civil War battlefield superintendents to obtain their perspectives, and what I discovered was fascinating. Approximately half urged caution as they did not traditionally interpret the aftermath of a battle to current times, (just what occurred on the battlefield and the principals involved). The other half stated it was time to change the paradigm, connect the historical dots, and talk about the war's aftermath and impact on race relations and related interests.

In the end, I got back to my headquarters colleague to report that "Civil War to civil rights" would be supported in the Southeast Region. With this in mind, my very able and capable staff began developing publications and products designed to reflect these interests with accompanying posters that were sent to many school districts around the country. These included "Slavery: Cause and Catalyst of the Civil War," "Hispanics and the Civil War: From Battlefield to Homefront," and "Native Americans in the Civil War."

Do you recall during my time at Appomattox Court House when I questioned what role my Latino ancestors had played during the Civil War? Well, I would finally get my answer over twenty years later! More than 20,000 Latinos fought in the Civil War, some for the Union and some for the Confederacy. Thousands of Latino civilians lent hearts and hands on the homefront.

Our publication, "Hispanics and the Civil War: From Battlefield to Homefront," provides a glimpse into some of the lives, stories, and achievements of Hispanics who fought and struggled for a more perfect Union. From the opening shots at Fort Sumter, South Carolina, to the final actions at Palmito Ranch near Brownsville, Texas, in 1865, many Hispanics chose to fight for the cause of either the Union or Confederacy for a variety of reasons.

Former Secretary of the Interior Ken Salazar stated in the publication, "The Sesquicentennial of the Civil War is a time to

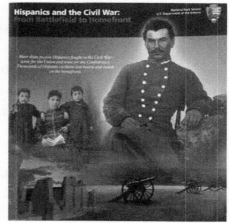

Hispanics and the Civil War: From Battlefield to Homefront, NPS Publication

commemorate those who fought and died during this pivotal era in American history. At the same time, it is an opportunity for us to renew our commitment to the ongoing march for freedom and equality for all people."

The publication received second place in the Short Book category during the National Association for Interpretation 2012 Media Awards Competition. I recall another Civil War-related experience that I will not soon forget.

Many years of growing tensions and strife between the North and South would erupt into civil war on April 12, 1861. Confederate artillery would fire upon the federal fort in Charleston Harbor, and Fort Sumter surrendered thirty-four hours later. Today, Fort Sumter remains a memorial to all who fought to hold on to it.

Approximately 200 invited guests would join me and Melissa at an event commemorating the 150th anniversary of the first shots of the Civil War on April 12, 2011. As we disembarked the ship connected to the Fort Sumter dock, period re-enactors representing soldiers as well as the home-front, along with a color guard provided by The Military College of South Carolina (The Citadel), led a precession with flags waiving as we headed into the historic fort.

As the senior NPS representative, an overwhelming sense of pride came upon me along with the tears. As I walked behind the precession, I found myself giving thanks to all who had prepared me for this moment, and who found it in their hearts to guide and support my career interests as I was now part of an historic event.

The ceremony reflected on the events of 150 years ago that sparked a war that cost over 620,000 American lives. It also recognized how our nation has emerged from the war and how we continue to be shaped by those events today.

"Four million enslaved African Americans saw [the Civil War] as their revolution," said Bob Sutton, former Chief Historian for the National Park Service. "Today we commemorate the beginning of the Civil War, but we also celebrate the fact that more people were freed from slavery at that time than at any time in world history."

Former NPS Director, Bob Stanton, and then Senior Advisor to Interior Secretary Ken Salazar, recalled the words of Frederick Douglass. "If he were here, he would remind us that we differ as the waves, but we are one as the sea," said Stanton. "We are one people, one nation, because we are indeed one as the sea."

As I gazed upon all who were in attendance and reflected upon what had occurred on the hallowed grounds of this historic fort, I remarked, "Through events and programs held throughout the country, it is our hope that the citizens of this nation will be challenged to consider how their lives, and their own American experience, have been shaped by this signature period of American history. For it is a shared history, and a shared legacy, owned by all. This era in American history should provide pause and reflection as the history and legacy of the American Civil War is owned and shared by all citizens of this great nation."

I had the opportunity to become involved, learn more about my own Latino heritage, and actively participate as the regional director in events surrounding the 450th anniversary of the founding of the first permanent European settlement in the United States.

St. Augustine, Florida, was founded in 1565 by Spanish explorer Admiral Pedro Menendez de Aviles. The Castillo de San Marcos fort symbolizes the Spanish heritage of St. Augustine and of the nation. Castillo de San Marcos National Monument is a unit of the National Park Service.

The St. Augustine 450th Commemoration Commission was established to ensure a suitable national observance of the 450th anniversary of the city of St. Augustine; cooperate with and assist in the programs and activities of the State of Florida in observance of the 450th anniversary of St. Augustine; assist in ensuring that the St. Augustine 450th anniversary observances were inclusive and appropriately recognized the experiences of all peoples in St. Augustine's history; and serve other tourism, international, resources, and economic interests.

The prospect of large amounts of oil washing up on NPS lands was nowhere on my radar screen until the Deepwater Horizon incident occurred on April 20, 2010, in the Gulf of Mexico. The oil spill was an industrial disaster and is considered to be the largest marine oil spill in petroleum industry history. After an estimated total discharge of 4.9 million barrels, the well was declared sealed on September 19, 2010.

Regarded as one of the largest environmental disasters in American history, it clearly was the focus and had the attention of the Department and the NPS, and valuable lessons were learned in the event of any future occurrences.

Two very significant and important milestones occurred in the Southeast Region: the seventy-fifth anniversary of Great Smoky Mountains National Park and the seventy-fifth anniversary of the Blue Ridge Parkway. The Smoky's events commemorated and highlighted the park's biologically diverse natural resources, cultural history, and recreational and educational opportunities.

On September 2, 2009, longtime park supporter, country music legend, and actress Dolly Parton did a magnificent job in celebrating the place and the stunning landscape that have made her what she is today.

Author with Mrs. Dolly Parton, Great Smoky Mountains NP, 2009,
NPS Photo

In a special edition magazine for the Great Smoky Mountains National Park seventy-fifth anniversary, Dolly stated, "The Smoky Mountains have inspired me and my music since I was a little girl." She added, "They touch my soul and lift my spirits. Let's celebrate America's most popular national park, but most especially, join me in making sure its magnificent beauty thrives for generations to come." Following the program, it was my honor to have the opportunity to thank her for all of her support.

The Parkway's renowned scenic byway celebrated its seventy-fifth anniversary on September 10-12, 2010, commemorating its first twelve-miles of construction at Cumberland Knob Recreation Area in North Carolina just south of the Virginia state line. For 469 miles, the slow-paced and relaxing drive along the Blue Ridge Parkway reveals stunning long-range vistas and close-up views of the rugged mountains and surrounding landscapes as well as the culture and history of the Appalachian Highlands.

(L/R, First Row, second person) 15th Director Robert (Bob) Stanton, 8th Director Ronald H. Walker, the author, 16th Director Fran P. Mainella, and 9th Director Gary Everhardt, Clemson University, 2012, Vela Family Photo

The Clemson University Institute for Parks recognizes exemplary leaders for their work in addressing environmental issues and concerns in parks and protected areas. I was honored as the recipient of the 2012 Robert G. Stanton Award "for sustained and innovative achievement in promoting racial and ethnic diversity in the management of North America's natural, historic, and cultural heritage" held at Clemson University during the George B. Hartzog, Jr. (seventh Director of the National Park Service) Environmental Awards Program.

The award is named in appreciation of Director Stanton's remarkable career as well as the expansion of the interpretation of diverse cultural meanings inherent in national parks and increased participation by racial and ethnic minorities.

Oh, I almost forgot about *Flipper!* While I was on an official trip visiting Biscayne National Park as well as park staff, the superintendent and chief ranger took me on a boat tour of this fascinating marine sanctuary. With clear blue skies and emerald-colored waters, there was something familiar to me about this special place. It was as if I had been on these waters before—which I had not. Then something occurred to me. I asked the superintendent if he recalled the television show *Flipper.* He replied that he had, and it was filmed in this area. Wow, the backdrop to the television show of my youth, a show that had inspired me to pursue a career in the outdoors, was present before me.

After nearly five years of some amazing experiences and adventures, yet another NPS director would provide me with an opportunity to expand upon some of the work we were doing for the youth, workforce, and diversity interests in the Southeast Region but on a much larger stage.

*Southeast Regional Office Leadership Team—(L/R)
Donna Losson, Gordon Wissinger, author, Ericka
Blevins, Gayle Hazelwood, and Shawn Benge, 2014,
Vela Family Photo*

With the creation of a new directorate—the Associate Director for Workforce, Relevancy and Inclusion, Melissa and I were heading back to our nation's capital.

CHAPTER 17

THE MOUNTAINS ARE CALLING

Never would I have imagined that I would walk past my new office nearly thirty years after the Medal of Honor ceremony on our way to meet NPS director Russ Dickenson, nor that from that visit as a cooperative education student striving to obtain a permanent position in the National Park Service, I would become the new Associate Director for Workforce, Relevancy, and Inclusion in Washington, DC.

Upon arrival at my new post, I had the same sense of excitement as when I entered the director's corridor at the Main Interior Building as a visitor in 1981. However, on this trip, I was not a visitor but an employee heading to my new office. My task was to create a new directorate designed to prepare the agency for a second century of service. This involved ensuring that our workforce reflected the face of America and that we promoted diversity and inclusion opportunities in all that we did as an agency.

From the stories that we told, workforce practices, to internal employee learning and development opportunities, the directorate was going to help make the business case and work with all parks and program offices to achieve the agency's mission and interests. In the process and for the first time in its history, these interests would have a permanent and sustained presence at the highest levels of our organization and in the director's corridor.

Upon working with NPS Director Jon Jarvis, the eighteenth Director of the National Park Service, and his leadership team over a period of two years, there was word on the streets that the superintendent of Grand Teton National Park was retiring. Upon hearing the news, I could not wait to tell Melissa that the post of superintendent of one of the first national parks that I had visited as a kid was now available.

Although I was thoroughly enjoying my job and the opportunity to promote and help institutionalize a diverse, relevant, and inclusive culture in the National Park Service, the very thought of serving as a senior executive superintendent of a large western national park was enticing, especially during the centennial celebration of the National Park Service. With the support of agency leadership, we were heading back to our park roots.

Now having both Washington (headquarters) and regional office experience behind me, to include three previous superintendent positions, Melissa and I were ready for the long cross-country drive to Moose, Wyoming. The journey in and of itself was an adventure, but what awaited us was totally unexpected.

The majestic snow-covered peaks of the Grand Teton range soon came into view on a beautiful day in March 2014. And just as millions of park visitors before us, taking a picture at one of the park's main entrance signs was a must. Melissa even did the high jump photo, but this aging park ranger with a bad back, hip, and knees was not going to attempt the maneuver despite my excitement upon arriving to my new post.

One of the first emotions that I had upon arriving for the first time in over forty years was a sense of awe and pride in the knowledge that I was now responsible for one of our National Park System's crown jewels. My

Arrival at Grand Teton National Park, 2014
Vela Family Photo

mind began to flash back to all of the NPS job experiences we'd had and all the communities we had worked in to get us to this special place and moment in time—San Antonio, Appomattox, Philadelphia, Brownsville, Austin, Johnson City, Atlanta, and Washington, DC.

It had been seven years since I had worked in a national park unit; it was a great feeling and brought a sense of belonging. It soon became apparent upon entering my new office, with windows framing the Grand Teton, that I was not in Washington, DC, any longer.

Snow, and lots of it, covered the landscape, and it was very cold as well. The park had experienced record levels of snowfall. Although Melissa and I had experienced snow over my career, this was going to be a different experience for two Latino country kids from Southeast Texas.

From our park community (employees, volunteers, concessioners, friends' group and donors, cooperating association, partners, and stakeholders) to the local community of Jackson, we were openly embraced and welcomed from the moment of our arrival.

The town of Jackson reminds me of a Western movie set, and the residents of this community are truly passionate, vocal, and active in protecting their national park—a great benefit to a superintendent. They also actively support park philanthropy and educational interests through the Grand Teton National Park Foundation and the Grand Teton Association.

With the goal of connecting with and creating the next generation of park visitors, supporters, and advocates as part of the commemoration of the National Park Service Centennial, Grand Teton National Park created a unique relationship with the local 2016 high school graduating seniors over a four-year period. We adopted the incoming freshman classes from Jackson Hole and Summit High Schools in 2012 with the intent of engaging and exposing them to the park and the National Park Service.

Students participated in many special initiatives and learning opportunities during our four-year relationship, such as attending a NPS Career Day to meet park scientists, interpreters, climbing rangers, and a variety of other occupations, as well as learning about the ecology and history of the park.

We provided scholarships and after-school internship opportunities, and several students served as "ranger club mentors" and provided leadership for an after-school club for younger students. Excursions were provided for students to explore scientific data needed to manage park resources, as well as activities that created a deeper appreciation and understanding of stewardship and wilderness principles.

I had the honor of serving as the keynote speaker during the Jackson Hole High School commencement ceremony. I stated in my remarks, "It is truly a grand celebration and honor to be involved with the graduating class of 2016. These remarkable young adults are beginning a new journey, and we encourage them to explore their heritage reflected in National Park Service sites and stories across the country, and always know they are welcome to their home park." The four-year program that the high school students completed was sponsored in part by the Grand Teton Association.

As the park's new superintendent, I quickly realized that preserving and protecting as well as providing for the needs of the millions of visitors who came to the park was something that we could not do alone. Thankfully, the Grand Teton

Author, Jenny Lake Renewal Project Ribbon-Cutting Ceremony, 2019, Vela Family Photo

Leslie Mattson, President, Grand Teton National Park Foundation, Vela Family Photo

113

National Park Foundation and the Grand Teton Association were valued partners of the park.

Having the opportunity to celebrate and cut the ribbon with Leslie Mattson, President of the Grand Teton National Park Foundation, in 2019 for the completed Jenny Lake Renewal Project was a great accomplishment for the Foundation, park staff, and our partners and donors. Nearly 1.9 million people visit Jenny Lake each year, making this historic landmark the park's most frequented visitor destination.

The Jenny Lake Renewal Project was a public-private partnership construction project that has restored one of Grand Teton National Park's most iconic visitor destinations while addressing deferred maintenance and accessibility at Jenny Lake. The $18 million project was funded by both the National Park Service ($4 million) and Grand Teton National Park Foundation ($14 million).

The Antelope Flats acquisition was one of the most important acquisitions in the park's history and was made possible through the successful completion of an eight-month fundraising campaign by the Grand Teton National Park Foundation

(L/R) Author in uniform; NPS director Jon Jarvis; Leslie Mattson, president, Grand Teton National Park Foundation; and Will Shafroth, president/ ceo of the National Park Foundation, 2016, Grand Teton National Park Foundation Photo

and their amazing board of directors and resource council as well as the National Park Foundation.

On December 12, 2016, the National Park Service purchased 640 acres within Grand Teton National Park from the State of Wyoming. Having raised $23 million in private funds, they were matched by $23 million from the federal Land and Water Conservation Fund. Antelope Flats now protects critical wildlife habitat and migration routes, prevents private development, and maintains spectacular viewsheds.

Author and wife Melissa, Grand Teton National Park, 2017, following the acquisition of the Mormon Row Property, Vela Family Photo

Another significant acquisition by the Grand Teton National Park Foundation was the Moulton Ranch Cabins, the last privately-held piece of property in the iconic Mormon Row Historic District. As descendants of T. A. Moulton, one of the original pioneers who homesteaded the area in the early twentieth century, the owners Hal and Iola Blake listed the property for sale in 2017.

A private purchaser could have redeveloped the inholding, building up to 10,000 square feet of new construction under Teton County, Wyoming's zoning regulations, and that may not have been compatible with the historic district and park's scenic viewshed.

As we arrived in our new community, I was surprised by the large number of Latinos living and working in the town of Jackson. I was equally disappointed at how seldom they visited the park, a fact I learned in conversations that Melissa and I would have with them in the community.

Author with participants of the "Pura Vida" program, Grand Teton National Park, 2018,
Vela Family Photo

The park is home to one of the most successful diversity youth engagement programs that I have ever seen in the National Park Service. Prior to my arrival, park staff had partnered with the Grand Teton National Park Foundation and the Teton Science Schools to create "Pura Vida," an outreach program that educates and engages Latino youth in the park. In addition, the program provides outdoor learning and leadership training. This program serves as a national model for how to effectively engage diverse youth and communities of color.

The park also has a unique and effective way in engaging youth through its Junior Ranger Program. Entitled "The Grand Adventure," the program invites participants to "discover the amazing wildlife, geology, history, and ecosystem of Grand Teton National Park as you experience what it takes to be a Park Ranger!"

Grand Teton National Park,
Junior Ranger Activity Booklet,
NPS Photo

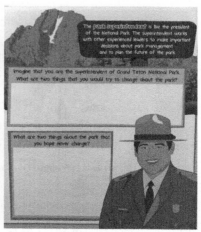

Author depicted in his role as
the park's superintendent,
NPS Photo

Author pinning on a Jr. Ranger badge, Grand Teton National Park, 2016,
Vela Family Photo

Park rangers provide a wide range of support to people in need. Whether it's rescuing stranded backcountry skiers in technical alpine terrain, assisting with vehicle accidents, or searching for a missing person, rangers are the first park responders.

Making Grand Teton National Park more inclusive and accessible within our facilities, programs, and projects was an ongoing priority and interest for me and my team. With these goals in mind, the park was recognized with the 2018 National Park Service Architectural Design Accessibility Achievement Award.

The award was given for superior accomplishments in advancing park opportunities for persons with disabilities at Jenny Lake. I was so very proud of our team and the Grand Teton National Park Foundation for their hard work and commitment in preserving and providing unencumbered and accessible access to the iconic landscape of Jenny Lake and the Teton Range through the Jenny Lake Renewal Project.

Founded in 1937, the Grand Teton Association is a 501 (c)3 nonprofit organization that has a long history of supporting education, interpretation, and research initiatives for their agency partners, including Grand Teton National Park.

Through their store sales, they provided a maximum return of store profits to the park while providing educational products and merchandise for park visitors.

As with Leslie Mattson and the Grand Teton National Park Foundation, I greatly valued and appreciated the support and

April Landale, Grand Teton Association Executive Director, Photo courtesy of the Grand Teton Association

partnership provided by April Landale, the Association's Executive Director, and all of those who came before her.

Her leadership and dedicated staff helped us to meet the visitor service and program needs of Grand Teton National Park. Our friendship, and all that the Association continues to do to support one of the crown jewels of the National Park System, is profoundly appreciated.

One of our other very valued partners is the Jackson Hole Airport. Located seven miles north of the town of Jackson, it serves as the only commercial airport located in a national park. The airport was established in the 1930s. Jim Elwood serves as the airport's executive director, and along with the airport board and his amazing staff, we worked closely to protect the natural environment while providing safe airline services across the country.

There were many challenges that the park had to address while serving and protecting this magnificent landscape and all of the visitors from around the world who came to enjoy it. I had many sleepless nights as my amazing workforce performed complex search-and-rescue missions involving visitor fatalities, plowing roads during blizzard conditions, managing wildland fires, and ensuring that millions of park visitors had a safe and memorable experience. This was all accomplished in an exceptional manner by our entire park team, volunteers, and partners.

Teton Interagency Firefighters were actively monitoring a lightning-ignited fire in Grand Teton National Park on the northwest side of Jackson Lake. The Berry Fire was detected on July 25, 2016, and burned a mixture of dead and down fuels and mature conifer forest. Park fire managers had anticipated lower than average fuel moisture combined with hotter and drier weather, which would continue to drive increased fire activity over the next few days.

Wildfire is an important and natural part of the Greater Yellowstone Ecosystem, as it helps to improve the overall health of the landscape by reducing fuel loads. In addition, fire releases nutrients back into the soil and creates new habitat for plants and animals.

When allowed to perform its natural role, fire has helped to shape the environment that park visitors see and enjoy today and influences the diversity of life found in the park. Despite our best fire modeling and forecasting, the fire more than doubled in size, thereby closing Highway 89, which leads to the south entrance of Yellowstone National Park, and also threatened park concession facilities and personnel.

In addition, the fire spread into the Bridger-Teton National Forest and the John D. Rockefeller Jr. Memorial Parkway. Aircraft, boats, fire tanker support vehicles, and additional fire personnel were mobilized to address the expanding fire. I had the opportunity to observe all of the fire activity by helicopter, and it was a surreal experience. Also, seeing the intense glow of the fire by vehicle and watching it jump across the road are not experiences I will soon forget. The roar of the fire will be lodged in my memory forever too. It was naturally extinguished that winter season.

Having served in three previous superintendent positions, I can unequivocally say that this is one complex park to manage. From the development of complex planning documents, management of $1 billion dollars in physical assets, to over 4.3 million visitors annually, this is truly a special place.

As a former regional director, I had reviewed and approved a number of planning and compliance documents, Environmental Impact Statements, and Environmental Assessments. However, what we were pursuing at Grand Teton would consume all of our efforts, talents, and patience.

The Moose-Wilson Road is narrow and winding, providing access to the south end of Grand Teton National Park. In addition, it offers a rustic, slow-driving experience for visitors looking for exceptional opportunities to view and enjoy wildlife and scenery. We needed to take a comprehensive look and create a long-term vision to address the significant issues facing the corridor such as traffic congestion, bicyclist safety, resource protection interests, and the visitor experience.

Our plan was developed by an interdisciplinary planning team led by the National Park Service. Four cooperating agencies, which included the Western Federal Lands Highway Division of the Federal Highway Administration, the State of Wyoming, Teton County, and the Town of Jackson, provided valuable input and perspectives during the planning process.

My staff also consulted and held onsite meetings with associated tribal representatives as well as with other federal, state, and local agencies and interested stakeholders as the plan was developed.

A final decision was reached for the Moose-Wilson Corridor Comprehensive Management Plan in December 2016. The plan is a testament to a three-year planning effort that began with the identification of the corridor's fundamental resources and values, the development of a range of alternatives for future management, and a comprehensive assessment of the environmental impacts associated with those alternatives. The selected path forward will balance preservation and public use and enjoyment within the corridor.

In addition, the intensity and timing of visitor use will be managed to provide high-quality visitor opportunities. Development within the corridor will generally be maintained within the existing footprint, thereby maintaining the outstanding and diverse natural ecosystem and cultural history of the area. The outcomes will reflect the care and concern people have for this special area within the park and the importance of devoting the time, effort, and patience to make it a reality.

The park experienced record visitation August 18–21, 2017, as visitors traveled to view a total solar eclipse. Park concession-operated campgrounds were near capacity, and for the first time in park history, all backcountry permits were issued for three days straight, the days leading to the solar eclipse.

In the course of preserving and protecting our national heritage, national parks are also economic engines and support local economies while enhancing the quality of life for park visitors and local residents. In 2019, 3.4 million park visitors spent an estimated $630 million in the local gateway regions while visiting Grand Teton National Park and supported a total of 8,640 jobs, $275 million in labor income, $463 million in value added, and $796 million in economic output in local gateway economies surrounding the park.

Working in national parks provides an opportunity to meet individuals of all backgrounds and life stories. Meeting the grandson of the first director of the National Park Service, Stephen Mather McPherson, was a true joy and experience. A successful industrialist, Stephen Mather decided to change course and pursue a career in public service.

Having called the secretary of the interior to voice his displeasure at how the national parks were being administered, he was invited to come to Washington.

Mather was appointed to lead the NPS, which was created within the Department of the Interior, where he served until 1929. Melissa and I had the opportunity to meet his grandson, Stephen Mather McPherson, his wife Tina, and members of his family at Jenny Lake Lodge.

We continued to enjoy our relationship as we tried to learn, honor, and live up to the examples and standards that Steve's grandfather left for the National Park Service. Little did I know how soon that was to occur.

Grand Teton National Park Leadership Team
(L/R first row) Gopaul Noojibail, Michael Nash, Donna Sisson, Vickie
Mates, Mallory Smith, Sue Consolo-Murphy, Denise Germann, author,
(L/R second row) Deborah Frauson, Mack McFarland, Daniel Noon,
Gary Pollock, Chris Finlay, and Jess Erwin, 2016,
NPS Photo

CHAPTER 18

A GRAND EXPERIENCE

It would be extremely difficult for me to capture all of the amazing experiences that occurred over the five years that I had served as the superintendent of Grand Teton National Park and as a park visitor. However, being bluff-charged by one of the park's most recognized grizzly bears is truly a memory that I will not soon forget!

Imagine that you live in a home where every room in the house provides a view that attracts millions of visitors each year. Melissa and I were truly blessed to wake up every morning in the superintendent's residence to the view of the Teton Range. And there were times when we would awake to the sounds of a huge bull elk feeding just outside our bedroom window with his antlers scrapping the sides of our house. We also experienced the sound of wolves at 3:30 am one morning and could see them plainly as a full moon illuminated the snow-covered landscape.

Although we had plans to travel and spend our first Christmas in 2014 with our kids and grandkids, the weather would have other plans. A large snow storm had hit our area, and we were forced to change our plans and spend

View from the author's living room,
the majestic Teton Mountain Range, 2014,
Vela Family Photo

Christmas by ourselves in Grand Teton National Park—not
a bad proposition. That was until we received a call from
John and Mary Kay Turner of the famed Triangle X Ranch.

Since 1926, the Turner Family has operated the Triangle
X Ranch within Grand Teton National Park, providing park
visitors with an authentic dude ranching experience. On that
Christmas day, we had the honor of spending Christmas
with the Turners.

Imagine a fire burning in a fireplace, family and friends
eating in the ranch's dining room, and then retiring to the
living room to hear holiday songs by John Turner and those
in attendance—with the Grand Teton in the foreground. What
a magical experience, and the beginning of a very valued
and lasting friendship and memory. And yes, it was a very
white and snowy Christmas. In 2016, the Ranch celebrated
its ninetieth anniversary.

Luci Baines Johnson, photo taken at the Murie Ranch, 2014
NPS Photo

I had the honor of hosting and participating in the fiftieth anniversary of the Wilderness Act in 2014. I invited my dear friend, Luci Baines Johnson, daughter of Lady Bird and President Lyndon Baines Johnson, to serve as our keynote speaker. The President had signed the bill into law in 1964, and nearly 350 people gathered on August 1, 2014, at Jackson Lake Lodge to celebrate the event.

The audience was delighted to hear lively stories about her mother and my friend, Lady Bird, and her life as the daughter of a larger-than-life U.S. President whose passion was "to build a great society, a place where the meaning of a man's life matches the marvels of man's labor."

Luci told those in attendance to "revel in the wonder of nature's grand symphony." She asked, "When another generation gathers to celebrate the Centennial of this great Act, will we be seen as the environment's heroes?" She went on to say, "The opposite of love is not hate ... and the opposite of life is not death; it's indifference. The wilderness—the beauty of our environment—is counting on each of us to escape the shackles of indifference."

(L/R) Luci Johnson, Melissa, author, and Lynda Robb near Grand Teton National Park, 2015,
Vela Family Photo

In her closing remarks, Luci made an appeal to act on behalf of wild lands and wild creatures and to heed "the rallying song of the 60s by the Beatles and 'come together, right now!'" She received a very big hug from a very proud superintendent as well as a well-deserved standing ovation from the audience.

Melissa and I thoroughly enjoyed our time together with Luci and her husband Ian Turpin. Ironically, she had many of the same park experiences that her mother had many decades ago. We also had the opportunity to all enjoy and spend time with Chuck and Lynda Robb and their family in Grand Teton National Park. It is a very valued friendship over fifteen years in the making.

If you ever want to have a chance to see grizzly bears or black bears in their native habitat, come to Grand Teton National Park. The park's bears are famous and even have web sites—I do not have one myself! Take for example, one such memory involving my dear friend and now retired Department of the Interior colleague Lynn McPheeters and her husband Jim from Virginia.

It was our custom to take house guests around the park to enjoy the scenery and wildlife, and we had an encounter with one of our renowned grizzly bears—#610 and her two cubs. In the late afternoon, we were driving toward Jackson Lake Dam when we spotted #610 and her two cubs heading toward the dam parking area, as had a number of other park visitors.

It is not uncommon for the park superintendent to be the first on the scene of a bear, moose, or elk jam involving park visitors and vehicles. When this occurs, I would try to keep visitors a safe distance so that they could take their pictures and maximize their visitor experience until the arrival of our trained and experienced volunteer wildlife brigade or law enforcement rangers.

As I was performing the task at hand (with Melissa, who is also a park volunteer), I recall thinking to myself that bear #610 is going to have to cross the road from the wooded area prior to reaching the dam parking lot. At that very instant, the bear was on the road, and we found ourselves in a brief staring contest.

I was close enough to see her expression and the color of her eyes! I had just one thought in mind: "Feet, don't fail me now!" As our eyes locked on each other, she made a bluff charge of a couple of feet, just enough to move us back so that her two cubs could join her in order to cross the street. Time literally stood still as I watched my life flash before my eyes.

As I recount this experience, my heart still races today, and I have had some sleepless nights all these years later.

There was a very popular movie involving a frontiersman on a fur trading expedition in the 1820s who fought for survival after being mauled by a bear and was left for dead by members of his own hunting team. Every time that I see that movie, I think about bear #610 and that brief but memorable encounter.

What I take away from this bear experience is the

Author's grandson, Nathaniel Vela, in the superintendent's office, Grand Teton National Park, 2017,
Vela Family Photo

motherly instincts that she had in protecting her cubs. She was doing what came naturally to her and just wanted to get our attention—she succeeded!

My heart would always skip a beat whenever I received a radio call from park dispatch or chief ranger Michael Nash after hours. Sadly, and during the over five years that I served as superintendent, we experienced multiple fatalities in the park.

Whether in excellent cardiovascular shape or an experienced climber, the impacts of weather, altitude, storms, and rockfalls were always a factor to consider in the Teton Mountain Range. For both experienced and unexperienced hikers and climbers, many were caught off-guard or did not have the stamina to deal with these unexpected challenges. Unfortunately, their decisions may have cost them their lives.

On my watch, four fatalities had occurred from 2014 to 2017 on the sixth highest peak in the Teton Range, Teewinot Mountain (12,330 feet). The name is derived from the Shoshone Native American word meaning "many pinnacles." The number of rescues and fatalities on Teewinot is much lower than the more popular Grand Teton. However, I always took each accident, near miss, and fatality personally, and with my team, tried to assess and learn from each incident.

However, there is one particular incident that is permanently seared into my memory. I had received a call from my then deputy superintendent Kevin Schneider (now superintendent of Acadia National Park and St. Croix Island International Historic Site).

One of my employees, Millie Jimenez, was returning from a hike in Avalanche Canyon with a friend late afternoon on October 12, 2015, when she lost her footing and fell onto a rocky slab. Having tumbled approximately twenty-five feet, she then fell another twenty feet, landing on a steep and rocky slope. Millie's hiking companion then called the Teton Interagency Dispatch Center from the scene.

Park rangers were flown to the area by helicopter and determined that she had sustained multiple serious injuries. Rangers promptly stabilized Millie and prepared her for aerial short-haul transport to an awaiting park ambulance at Lupine Meadows. Upon receiving the call from Kevin, Melissa and I rushed to Lupine Meadows where the helicopter was about to land and then followed the ambulance to the hospital where we accompanied her into an emergency room.

Although I always took any tragic incident personally, Millie's injury took it to an even higher level as she was my employee. No matter the incident, I was so very proud of our emergency response teams. Climbing rangers, park ambulance personnel, fire and search and rescue—they all did an amazing job saving lives, and that includes our dear friend, Millie. Although a painful recovery, she continues to experience and enjoy the backcountry and hiking.

Imagine cross-country skiing in the middle of the night, in the winter, with a full moon as a backdrop. One can have a full winter experience with no problem at 3:00 am in the morning with the moonlight glistening over a landscape covered in snow in Grand Teton National Park.

Whether on water or on land, we were fortunate to have these and many more memories and experiences with our family and friends. Grand Teton National Park is truly a spectacular place, and one of many experiences that await visitors to our national parks!

*Author's daughter Christina and
grandchildren, superintendent's residence,
2014, Vela Family Photo*

*Author's wife, Christina, grandchildren, and author, Snake River, 2014,
Vela Family Photo*

*Author and wife Melissa on Jackson Lake with Mt. Moran
in the background, Grand Teton National Park, 2016,
Vela Family Photo*

CHAPTER 19

"I DO SOLEMNLY SWEAR"

As I described in the previous chapters, the Grand Teton National Park Foundation gifts millions of dollars to the park each year. Throughout the year, I would attend donor events around the country with the Foundation's President, Leslie Mattson. After attending a couple of events, and with the support of her amazing staff, we developed a pretty effective routine, and a lasting friendship. I would provide an operational update on the affairs and interests of the park while Leslie would expertly provide an explanation of park needs and donor opportunities.

During a donor trip to California on April 10, 2018, and having just landed in Salt Lake City with Melissa, I received a call on my cell phone from the Secretary of the Interior's office. The caller indicated that Secretary Zinke wanted to visit with me in his office and how long would it take to travel to Washington.

Upon concluding our donor event, I traveled to our nation's capital, and on April 16, 2018, I was ready to meet the secretary. Upon greeting Secretary Zinke, he asked if I knew why he had called me to his office. I replied, "how can I be of assistance?"

One of the first questions that the secretary asked was, "How can we fix the National Park Service?" Without any hesitation, I replied that we needed to build the next generation of conservation stewards and workforce with diversity as a focus, address growing morale issues, aggressively tackle our expanding maintenance backlog, and maintain a culture of ethics and excellence. In addition, I shared with Secretary Zinke what my amazing management team at Grand Teton was achieving in order to address the issues that I had just raised.

I was being interviewed to be the next director of the National Park Service! I was in agreement with the secretary's interests for the NPS, and at the conclusion of the meeting, was told that a follow-up interview may be needed at the White House as the secretary would be meeting with other potential candidates. The interview with White House staff occurred on June 22, 2018.

On a subsequent trip to visit my parents in Wharton, Texas, as well as to see remodeling efforts to their home that had been damaged during a hurricane a year earlier, Melissa happened to glance at the White House nomination web site.

While doing so, she let out a yell that we had been nominated! I can not adequately put into words the excitement in our house, and after giving Melissa a big bear hug, I turned my attention to my parents. With tears in our eyes, I told my parents that this day was possible because of that very special trip that we made to Yellowstone and because of all their love and support.

On August 31, 2018, the official White House posting read: "President Donald J. Trump Announces Intent to Nominate and Appoint Personnel to Key Administration Posts—Raymond David Vela of Texas, to be Director of the National Park Service, Department of the Interior." I was poised to serve as the nineteenth director of the National Park Service, and the first Latino to be nominated in the agency's over one-hundred-year history. Oh, how my world would change!

Written on White House stationary, the letter dated September 6, 2018, stated, "The Office of Presidential Personnel has enjoyed working with you throughout the selection and clearance processes. As you are aware, the President submitted your nomination to the Senate to fulfill their role of advice and consent. Congratulations and best wishes for a speedy confirmation."

A statement released by Secretary Zinke said, "David Vela has demonstrated all of the ideals that the National Park Service stands for, and his long track record of leadership on behalf of the people and places of the National Park Service distinguish him as the right man for the job."

Melissa and I always envisioned that Grand Teton National Park would be our last duty station, since we cared deeply for the park, my staff, partners, and the Jackson Hole community. Therefore, it would take the prospect of serving as the next director for us to leave this majestic place.

The preparation that would be needed prior to my confirmation hearing before the Committee on Energy and Natural Resources in the United States Senate during the 115th Congress on November 15, 2018, would be one of the most intense and challenging in my over thirty-eight years of public service, and one of the most exhilarating.

The first order of business was to work on getting briefed on the Department and NPS priorities and operational interests; develop briefing statements; and meet with senators on the committee as well as those who wanted to meet with the nominee.

Having watched Senate confirmation hearings on television over the years, I always wondered what went on behind the scenes, and I would soon find the answer to that question.

In addition to the Hill visits, much time was spent on responding to a required Senate questionnaire, developing and reading briefing statements, and preparing for a mock hearing, which is affectionally known as a "murder board" comprised of senior leaders and attorneys in the Department. For two hours, I was grilled on everything from my views on climate change, our deferred maintenance interests, and the most pressing needs of the National Park Service. Now mentally and physically exhausted, I was ready!

With family and friends from Texas and Jackson Hole in attendance, Chairman Lisa Murkowski of Alaska gaveled the hearing to order. A total of three nominees would testify at the hearing: a nominee to serve as the assistant secretary of Energy, another to serve on the Federal Energy Regulatory Commission, and me as the nominee for director of the National Park Service.

It was a packed hearing room, with some demonstrators in attendance. There was speculation that the other two nominees would get the majority of the questions in light of previously perceived controversial statements and or actions taken. However, I would soon discover that this was not the case.

Chairman Murkowski stated, "Mr. Vela has been nominated to be the director of the National Park Service. He would oversee some of our greatest national treasures. In order to ensure that our parks are here for future generations, we must balance our ability to enjoy and explore them with our responsibility to keep and maintain them. If he is confirmed, he will be responsible for leading the way in finding that balance. It is also expected that he would take on a wide range of issues facing the Park Service, from sexual harassment to the deferred maintenance backlog. I think it is significant to note that he would be the first Hispanic American confirmed to this position."

Ranking Member Maria Cantwell of the State of Washington stated, "The National Park Service has been without a confirmed director for nearly two years. I am very pleased that the President has finally nominated someone for this important position. I am especially pleased that he has nominated someone who has come up through the Park Service ranks. Mr. Vela has been a park ranger, a park superintendent, and he should understand the problems that face our parks firsthand."

Melissa, our kids, grandkids, relatives (to include my Uncle Paul and Aunt Gennie Vela, as well as my cousin Bianca), friends, and colleagues were sitting behind me with cameras rolling in front of us. Melissa was sitting to my left shoulder with our grandson Xavier to my right. In front of each nominee was a microphone and a red button indicating it was time to end our responses to a question.

Melissa was receiving real-time text messages from family and friends around the country indicating that she needed to move slightly from one side or another in order to be seen by

Author and wife Melissa
prior to hearing, 2018,
Vela Family Photo

Author, Senate hearing
swearing-in, 2018,
Senate Hearing Photo

Author's family at committee hearing, 2018,
Vela Family Photo

the cameras. In addition, and on one particular question, Xavier noticed that my light had turned red and whispered into Melissa's ear (who is known by the grandkids as Mimi) that grandpa "is over his time and needs to wrap it up."

Each nominee had a senator who provided a brief supporting statement. I had the honor of having a fellow Texan, the Honorable John Cornyn, serve in this capac-

Author with Dr. Scott Shafer and wife Mrs. Debe Shafer, 2018, Vela Family Photo

ity. In his remarks, Senator Cornyn stated, "His extensive experience and dedication to public service have prepared him to confront the many challenges, and there are many challenges confronting the National Park Service." I was truly humbled and honored by his remarks, and it was now time for my opening statement.

After saying a quick prayer in my head, I began. "As the oldest grandchild of a sharecropper, my journey through the National Park Service began on a trip to Yellowstone National Park while a young teenager from our rural home in Wharton, Texas. My parents decided one day to take a trip with my younger brother Michael, sister Judy and I, and it proved to be a journey of a lifetime."

I continued, "The image of that National Park Ranger truly caught my eye, and I began to think about how special it must be to work in a national park. Upon arriving home from Yellowstone, I devoured every article that our assistant high school librarian, Mrs. Betty Bergstrom, could find."

I also stated, "I have had the honor of working with a very passionate and dedicated workforce—the pride of the National Park Service. I am so very proud of our permanent, seasonal, and volunteer workforce. Yet, we as an agency have fallen short in treating them with the dignity and respect that they truly deserve. The scourge of sexual and workplace harassment in society and in the National Park Service must stop! Great strides have been made within the agency, but there's more to be done. If confirmed, I will continue to hold people and processes accountable to ensure that we achieve our workplace and workforce interests."

I concluded my opening statement by saying, "As the first Latino in the over 102-year history of the National Park Service to be nominated as director, I am reminded of the lessons taught to me by a sharecropper; be humble, maintain a strong moral and ethical compass, and pursue causes greater than myself ... if confirmed, I eagerly look forward to working with you in protecting what has been called 'America's Best Idea,' our nation's national parks."

Soon afterward, the questions began in earnest. Throughout the hearing, I was becoming more and more comfortable and confident that all of the hours of preparation, briefing statements, and the "murder board" was paying off. A clear indication of how things were going was the number of invitations I had received from senators on the committee to visit their states once confirmed as director.

There was one particular question asked by Louisiana Senator Bill Cassidy that got a good laugh from both me and those in attendance. With a serious expression, Senator

Cassidy asked, "Mr. Vela, a critical question [as he was asking his question, I quickly began thinking about our park units in Louisiana and major issues that he would ask me]. In two weeks, LSU plays Texas A&M. Whom will you support?" I stated in response, "Very good question, sir. Today, it is LSU." The senator then replied, "Oh my gosh, I am all for it—although I will doubt his veracity."

I should probably stop now and beg for forgiveness to all of my fellow Texas A&M alumni and Aggie nation for my response. But I really needed the senator's vote! But do not worry, Ags, as fellow Texas A&M graduate Dr. Scott Shafer quickly brought me back down to reality after the hearing!

Before I knew it, the hearing was over. As soon as the gavel came down adjourning the hearing, I had this tremendous rush of emotions. I gave Melissa an emotional bear hug after congratulating my fellow nominees on their testimony.

After taking family pictures, which included each of our grandkids sitting in the chair that I had just used for the hearing, we treated all of our guests to a big Texas barbecue lunch at a local Washington, DC, restaurant.

The United States Senate Committee on Energy and Natural Resources met on November 27, 2018, at 10:00 am to hold their business meeting for the purpose of voting on the three nominees. In a near unanimous vote, my nomination was forwarded to the senate for confirmation. Upon a month of waiting, and Melissa and I spending many long hours in the senate gallery waiting for a vote, the 115th Congress ended without approving my and many other nominations that had cleared their respective senate committees.

CHAPTER 20

END OF SHIFT

Hopeful but needing to be renominated by the President during a new congress, and having left Grand Teton National Park for the last time, I was recommended by the then-acting director of the National Park Service, P. Daniel (Dan) Smith, to serve as the permanent deputy director for operations for the National Park Service in Washington, DC. The recommendation was approved by the department on September 12, 2019.

As Deputy Director for Operations, I managed all National Park System Units in addition to a group of national programs that supported the efforts of others to preserve natural and cultural resources and to enhance recreational opportunities in places not administered by the

The author with Dan Smith, First African Landing Commemorative Weekend, Fort Monroe National Monument, 2019, Vela Family Photo

National Park Service. I was now officially and permanently back in Washington, DC.

By this time, Secretary Zinke had been replaced by his deputy secretary, David Bernhardt, who was confirmed as the fifty-third secretary of the interior on April 11, 2019. Participating in senior-level management team meetings, providing briefings to the assistant secretary for fish and wildlife and parks and the deputy secretary on departmental goals, and helping to manage the daily affairs with acting director Smith was the order of the day—until coronavirus disease 2019 (COVID-19). Our world, and that of the nation, would change forever.

One of my principal duties was to maintain and enhance partnerships at every level of government, Our founding director believed that the states and the federal government needed to work together to develop a great national system of parks. Our nation's state parks help to preserve a rich tapestry of natural and cultural history and provide recreational opportunities that enrich the quality of life of their residents and visitors. In addition, they are an extremely valuable and strategic partner of the National Park Service. In 2019, I had the honor of addressing the National Association of State Park Directors (NASPD) Conference in Rogers, Arkansas.

After coming out of retirement to join the new Administration, and upon working for twenty-one months, Acting Director Smith (whose official title was Deputy Director, Exercising the Authority of the Director), decided to leave his post. He then served as a senior advisor to the director and national commemorations manager.

Through secretarial order, Secretary Bernhardt would then appoint me to serve as the Deputy Director, Exercising the Authority of the Director of the National Park Service. Secretarial Order Number 3345, Amendment Number 29, dated September 30, 2019, stated, "This Order is intended to ensure uninterrupted management and execution of the duties of these vacant non-career positions during the presidential transition pending senate-confirmation of new non-career officials."

Through this action, a young Latino kid from Wharton, Texas, who dreamed of one day wearing the iconic "green and gray" uniform was now in charge of the National Park Service. I had a range of emotions sitting for the first time in the director's office as a flood of emotions entered my mind on my first day in office. All of the moves that Melissa and I had made, plus hard work, faith, and believing that I could one day accomplish my ultimate objective, this dream had now come true.

On my first day in the job on October 1, 2019, I sent an email message with an accompanying video to the entire workforce of the National Park Service entitled, "The Beginning of a Second Century Conversation." The message stated, "Dear NPS Family, on my first full day as Deputy Director, exercising the authority of the director, I wanted to speak with you directly and share with you what we are doing here in Washington to prepare, support, and empower our workforce for

Acting director of the National Park Service, 2019
Vela Family Photo

a second century of service. This is the first of many conversations I look forward to having with you in the coming months. Thank you, as always, for your continued stewardship of our park resources and dedication to serving those who come to enjoy them."

The video was filmed on the steps of the Lincoln Memorial near the location of Dr. Martin Luther King, Jr's "I Have a Dream Speech." While looking over the National Mall toward the Washington Monument, I shared a brief synopsis of our vision for a second century of service. However, the stark reality of COVID quickly absorbed my attention.

Working with my amazing leadership team and staff of the United States Public Health Service, which has been a part of the NPS for over one hundred years, we began the process of understanding COVID—what was it, how was it spread, what was the impact to park employees, our partners, and the many millions of park visitors?

Upon creating a national incident management team(s), we began the work of developing an adaptive management strategy for our leaders in the field, working from guidance provided by the Centers for Disease Control and local and state public health authorities. This involved modifying our operations for facilities and programs, including closing them when necessary.

Although I understood the department's desire to quickly open as many facilities as we could to help offer economic and recreational health benefits, I did not always agree with the approach on how to safely achieve these interests, especially considering the emotional appeals of tribal and local communities who could not sustain the potential medical needs and impacts of park visitation within their communities. I was also dismayed by the number of people who dismissed state governors' "stay at home" and local public health orders in order to visit national parks, for purely recreational purposes, that were many states away.

In response to numerous media inquiries and news releases, I advised visitors that they should prepare themselves for a "new normal" that will not likely square with their last national park visit. In addition, I said, "You may have facilities that aren't going to be available, but the (park's) footprint will be. So, it will be a different visitor experience, and it will be a different normal that we're going to need to own and, frankly, mitigate."

I also stated, "This gets to the value and importance of making sure that visitors know what to expect when they get to the park, making sure that visitors go to the park's website (and) social media ... as to what is accessible, how to plan your trip, and, most importantly, what are the expectations when you get there."

Even while working through a global pandemic, there were moments of pride and reflection. My acting Deputy Director for Operations, Shawn Benge, came up with the idea of rotating park superintendents into the director's office to work directly with NPS leadership on everything from obtaining COVID park updates to communicating our decisions to regional directors and park superintendents.

One such superintendent was Robin Snyder, who manages both Appomattox Court House National Historical Park and Booker T. Washington National Monument. Approximately sixty miles apart, the two parks tell the story of Civil War to civil rights. All of the superintendents did a magnificent job in performing their detail assignments.

Author's wife Melissa and Robin Snyder, Washington, DC, 2019,
Vela Family Photo

What makes Robin's story unique was that she is a native of Appomattox, Virginia, and was taught seventh grade keyboarding by my wife, Melissa Vela! Robin later graduated from Appomattox High School and attended the University of Virginia, where she obtained a bachelor of arts in American History and a masters of education.

Wow, one of my wife's former students would work her way up the chain of command, and would later serve as the superintendent of the very park that we had left over thirty years ago. As you can imagine, it was quite the reunion.

I will always be profoundly grateful for the leadership and efforts provided by Shawn Benge, Acting Deputy Director for operations and our team in Washington, our incident commanders and regional directors, as well as Captain Sara

Newman and the dedicated men and women of the United States Public Health Service.

The consecutive work days and long hours put a strain on me and my small staff who were working in Washington during the COVID period, as well as those in the field who were not teleworking. Frankly, it impacted in one way or another our entire NPS workforce and strategic partners, as well as how we had to conduct our program responsibilities. In addition to addressing the demands of COVID, racial and social unrest in our nation's capital and around the country would have an impact on an already exhausted team.

The growing call to remove Confederate statues around the country, allegations of police violence centered around the death of George Floyd (a forty-six-year-old black man, who was killed in Minneapolis, Minnesota on May 25, 2020 while being arrested), which resulted in racial tensions and riots across the country, and the desecration of memorials would now require our attention—in addition to managing a large and complex federal agency.

The United States Park Police (USPP) are on the front lines during demonstrations that occur within the nation's capital and on the National Mall, handling everything from relatively small to very large and complex events throughout the year.

On June 13, 2020, the USPP issued the following statement: "In assisting the USSS (United States Secret Service) with their protective mission of the White House Zone, more than 50 U.S. Park Police Officers sustained injuries, some being hospitalized, throughout the operational period starting on May 29th. This illegal behavior by the protestors also resulted in several structure fires and significant property damage."

In addition, the statement said, "Following the violence that continued on May 30th where officers were hit with bricks and assaulted, the USSS and USPP had initial discussions regarding adjustments to the collective posture in Lafayette Park and potentially obtaining fencing. As violence and destruction continued in Washington, DC, putting both the public and law enforcement at risk, on Sunday, May 31, USSS confirmed with USPP that the anti-scale fencing would be procured and potentially delivered on Monday for installation along H Street. The installation of the fence proved to successfully limit the amount of assaults and injuries sustained by Force personnel. The amount of injuries dramatically decreased beginning June 2, 2020, throughout the rest of the week. It also allowed for time, space, and manner for those who wished to peacefully demonstrate."

Over the course of my years working in and around the nation's capital, I have experienced many peaceful demonstrations, whether impromptu or organized through the NPS permitting process. The vast majority were peaceful and respectful of law enforcement and public property. However, there are times when a criminal or individuals who do not respect the rule of law decide to become involved and pursue an agenda that is different than that of the demonstrators.

In response to the racial and social unrest throughout the country, I sent a statement regarding race, equity, and the values of the National Park Service to my workforce on June 9, 2020. Here are some excerpts from the statement: "Through their voices and actions, individuals across the nation and around the world are addressing racial injustices within the black community. As the stewards of parks who protect the sites and tell the stories of this ongoing struggle,

I want to convey our voice, the voice of the National Park Service. The National Park Service commits to lead change and work against racism. We are thoroughly committed to an ongoing and sustainable conversation with resulting products and outcomes for the benefit of current and future generations."

Throughout my NPS career, I have reviewed a number of demographic studies as to why people of color do not visit national parks compared to their white counterparts. In my opinion, travel costs to include entrance fees for low-income families, the lack of transportation, location (especially remote parks in the West), and safety are contributing factors.

I vividly recall hosting a diversity session at a national NPS conference decades ago when I asked an African American colleague his thoughts on the lack of visitation by his community. His response was compelling: "Because when my ancestors went into the woods, they did not always come out."

That profound statement forever changed my thinking and engagement strategies for communities of color, as a "one size fits all" strategy was not going to be effective.

The NPS had completed a ten-year demographic study on park visitation that ABC News wanted to discuss with me in addition to other representatives from diverse communities and outdoor organizations.

Our 419 national parks remained overwhelmingly white with just 23 percent of park visitors being people of color. With minorities making up 42 percent of the U.S. population, 77 percent of park visitors were white. During the course of my interview, and when confronted with our findings, my response was, "That tells me that we've got a lot of work to do."

In response to the question of removing Confederate statues in national parks, I stated, "If we do that on park land, we then remove the stories that they contain. And if those stories are further sanitized in the history text, we can—we may completely lose that narrative. We can't."

The reporter also referenced how park ranger uniforms resemble those worn by law enforcement and are intimidating to some immigrants and minorities in light of documented cases of profiling. My response was that I recognized that history and the fear it instills, and we are developing strategies to combat it. In addition, I said, "We have to be responsive to those needs ... because they're going to be different. And it's going to require a different approach. And so, we have to own that." I never forgot what I learned many decades ago from that diversity session and discussion with my African American colleague.

What began as a very reflective and important assessment of the value and importance of promoting and sustaining a quality, safe, and enriching park experience for all Americans was turned into political theater by a national television talk show host. The host stated that I should resign or be fired for interjecting race into a discussion about who visits national parks.

The television host completely lost why we perform demographic studies and what we can learn from them. At no time, and under no circumstances, would the NPS exclude any person or community of color from enjoying and experiencing what is our intrinsic American birthright—our nation's national parks—because of their race.

Sadly, it was this television host who chose to make visitation to our national parks a racial issue for his own political and partisan gain, as 77 percent of park visitors are white. The NPS has come a long way, but has much more to do to ensure that "America's best idea" is experienced and enjoyed by all.

Over 400 years ago, the first enslaved Africans were brought to English-occupied North America at Point Comfort, which is now part of Fort Monroe National Monument in Virginia. In August 2019, the nation paused to commemorate that moment in our nation's history and to honor their legacy.

Dan Smith and I joined the park's superintendent, Terry E. Brown, in providing remarks on behalf of the National Park Service. With over twenty-five years of federal service, superintendent Brown (African American) has done a great job in building knowledge and capacity within the surrounding communities about the rich history in the monument's footprint. Monument staff tell the story of the landing of the first enslaved Africans in English-occupied North America in 1619.

The National Park Service and the U.S. Semiquincentennial Commission (the federal body tasked with commemorating and celebrating the nation's 250th anniversary of independence) partnered to commemorate the 250th anniversary of the signing of the Declaration of Independence in 2026.

Working collaboratively, this partnership will enhance efforts to educate and inspire the nation during the largest and most inclusive commemoration in our nation's history. From July 4, 2020, and through July 4, 2026, the Commission and the NPS will work to connect nearly 350 million Americans, as well as millions of international friends, with our country's heritage and continuing journey to form a more perfect Union.

One of my duties as acting director was to serve as the chair for the Committee for the Preservation of the White

*Chair, Committee for the
Preservation of the White House,
2020,
Vela Family Photo*

*Author speaking at
a White House Rose Garden
Event, 2020,
Vela Family Photo*

House. The committee plays an advisory role and is charged with the preservation of the White House, the official home and principal workplace of the President of the United States.

Working with First Lady Melania Trump, who serves as the honorary chair of the committee, committee members as well as National Park Service and White House staff, we established policies relating to the museum function of the White House as well as made recommendations on acquisitions for the permanent collection.

I fondly recall my first meeting as chair, which was held in the President's Theater in the White House. Prior to calling the meeting to order, I reflected upon my early days while on a training assignment at Lyndon B. Johnson National Historical Park where I catalogued suits worn by President Johnson in the White House. I was now working with accomplished leaders in the fields of museum curation,

Melissa and Author, The White House, July 4th, 2020
Vela Family Photo

historic preservation, and architecture to preserve and protect the White House.

In celebrating our centennial year, we also embraced a second century of service. This new century had already challenged the status quo in ways that required us to chart a new normal in order to educate and inspire, as well as to serve and protect our nation's heritage.

With the support of my leadership team, we developed the NPSNext initiative, which re-evaluated and recommitted to a culture and organization that we needed in order to serve the interests of the Department and the NPS.

Working with our Washington office, we identified areas where our focus could bring about key changes. Our ultimate aim was to tap into the collective wisdom and passion of our workforce in order to align priorities and co-create an overarching vision for a second century.

On July 15, 2020, in an email to the NPS workforce entitled, "Guiding our Second Century of Service: Washington Support NEXT," I stated, "Our commitment to doing a better job of listening and building a genuinely more inclusive environment begins with us, the senior leadership team of the Washington Support Office, transparently sharing our own vision for the future, and the support we will provide to get there."

On many occasions during my career, I had the opportunity to speak to corporate officials, other government agencies at the state and federal level, and to academia. One of the highest honors that I had was being selected to speak at the George B. Hartzog, Jr. (seventh director of the National Park Service) Lecture Series in Park and Conservation Area Management at Clemson University.

The lecture series was developed to feature leading figures in the field of conservation. Adding to remarks that were made by many previous NPS directors, my talk was entitled, "NPS Next: The Second Century of the National Park Service" and was delivered on October 22, 2019.

In addition to the Hartzog Lecture Series, the annual Hartzog Awards program recognizes exemplary leadership in addressing environmental issues and concerns. I was honored with The Walter T. Cox Award for sustained achievement in public service providing leadership in administration of public lands and for policy formation affecting our natural and cultural resources.

The award is named for Dr. Cox's distinguished career in education and public service, especially during his tenure as President of Clemson University and as the director of the Santee-Cooper Authority.

Having the honor and privilege of managing the National Park Service was an opportunity of a lifetime, as was working with one of the best workforces in the entire federal government. However, after much prayer and conversations with Melissa and the kids, it was time for me to leave my beloved "green and gray."

I submitted my retirement letter to Secretary Bernhardt dated July 31,

The Author, Washington, DC,
End of Shift – August 29, 2020,
Vela Family Photo

2020, stating, "With the support of my wife of 40 years and my family, I have decided that it is time to hang up my Stetson for the last time effective September 30, 2020. One of my favorite quotes is from President Theodore Roosevelt when he stated, 'People don't care how much you know until they know how much you care.' It is my hope that my workforce will understand my decision and know that my passion and goal was always their safety and care."

With my father experiencing serious medical issues back home in Texas, I decided to leave earlier than planned and walked out of the Main Interior Building for the last time on August 29, 2020. I entered into retirement the following day, blessed and honored to have worked with a dedicated and passionate workforce, serving and protecting our nation's most special places.

"As the National Park idea flowered in this century, it produced a special kind of conservationist—the park ranger—who has made unique contributions to our understanding of the natural world and its relationship to our future well-being."
—*Stewart L. Udall, former secretary of the interior*

CHAPTER 21

TEACHABLE MOMENTS

O ver the course of my thirty-eight years of public service at the state and federal level, there were many teachable moments, great joys, and challenges. I was often asked, "How can we be more successful in what we do?" My answer was consistent—be more relevant, be more diverse, and be more inclusive, in what YOU do.

One of my favorite quotes is by Maya Angelou: "We all should know that diversity makes for a rich tapestry, and we must understand that all the threads of the tapestry are equal in value no matter what their color." As public servants, our ability to truly connect with those who we serve, whether through regulations and policies or public services, is dependent upon our ability to effectively respect, listen, and engage.

There was something that always bothered me, though, no matter what administration was in office. The vast majority of the 70,000 employees working in the Department of the Interior are dedicated career public servants with political appointees. There were times when I would hear political or appointed employees make comments such as, "Let's make sure our people are in the room," or "Let's make sure that our people are in the lead ..." And sometimes such appointed figures would say something like, "We can't trust them [career employees]" with a particular task or outcome. This was always hard for me to understand and accept.

For any administration, and regardless of party affiliation, my advice is to listen to your workforce, set clear expectations and realistic timeframes, give them the benefit of the doubt, and trust that their actions will be in keeping with laws, regulations, and policies.

With few exceptions, and in my over thirty years in the National Park Service, it did not matter what party affiliation an employee supported. What mattered was getting the job done while taking on causes greater than themselves.

It is equally important to assess and address the needs of a workforce and workplace. For example, there remains a lack of diversity within federal public land management agencies and a need to be more inclusive and relevant in the lives of all in this country.

There is also a general assumption that minorities do not participate in or support outdoor interests, and yet national surveys reveal otherwise. To the contrary, families of color are often seen in public parks, especially when picnic facilities are available for family gatherings nearby. Visitation to more remote national parks by people of color has traditionally been low but those travel dynamics are beginning to change.

As I recounted earlier, just one park experience had a profound and lasting impact on my life. With communities of color growing throughout the country, how could, or would, relevancy, diversity, and inclusion (RDI) influence the National Park Service in a second century of service? NPS directors faced these issues head-on during the Jim Crow and civil rights era right up to the current day with varying levels of success.

I recall the first time that I heard the term "RDI"; I had no clue as to its meaning, yet it was becoming clear that it was gaining momentum within public and private sectors. In whole or in parts, RDI is now being reflected within organizational structures and on more business cards in the federal government.

If I have learned anything about RDI it's that if an agency's culture and organizational DNA is not supportive, the chances of making significant change and impact are severely limited. An agency can effectively *talk* about RDI and have well-attended special events, but if the agency's culture and workforce does not embrace these initiatives and outcomes, they are usually short-lived.

Over the years, the NPS has struggled with a lack of diversity within its workforce, with approximately 80 percent of the permanent workforce being Anglo. I have some personal perspectives on this matter based on over thirty years of service in the NPS.

One of the most challenging conversations that we had involving RDI was during a National Leadership Council (NLC) meeting in Washington, DC. The NLC is comprised of the agency's political and career senior executives, deputy directors, and the director as well as selective staff.

The topic of this particular meeting was "institutional racism" within the National Park Service, and it was facilitated by then-political NPS deputy director Mickey Fearn (African American). Mickey has been a public servant and park and conservation professional for over fifty years. He is currently a professor of practice for the North Carolina State University's School of Natural Resources.

I recall one of my colleagues telling me prior to the meeting that he did not have a racist bone in his body and was insulted by the conversation that we were having. I agreed with his assessment regarding what he had done to advance the cause of diversity within the agency but reminded him that the conversation involved "institutional racism."

Needless to say, it was one of the most challenging and emotional conservations that I had experienced at the highest levels of the National Park Service. Director Jon Jarvis and deputy director Fearn took us out of our comfort zones and forced us to confront some of the most pressing issues facing the NPS, such as the question of how to make ourselves relevant to all segments of society while ensuring that our workforce reflected the face of the nation.

Although the NPS manages many of our nation's most special places and all of the stories that they contain, I can understand why communities of color could assume that the NPS does not embrace the tenants of relevancy, diversity, and inclusion as our lack of workforce diversity is noticeable.

Over the course of my NPS career, there were many occasions when I would serve as the first or only Latino to have occupied a particular leadership position within a park or in a room of colleagues. Today, there are a relatively small number of Latino and other minority NPS superintendents, and it would take 102 years for a Latino to be nominated to serve as the Director of the National Park Service.

There were also times when I felt that I was having to constantly prove that I was worthy of the job or task at hand.

In addition, I would feel compelled to address RDI interests in a meeting as it was not being discussed during a critical conversation.

However, and despite these challenges, I was able to grow and advance through the organization, confident in my abilities and thankful for my life experiences that served as my compass. I may owe that elderly gentleman who I had worked for as a teenager a debt of gratitude as in that difficult moment over forty-five years ago, I was so very proud of my heritage and left that experience with a burning desire to tackle whatever life threw my way.

The agency's culture and DNA began to change over the years as former NPS directors created urban areas and ethnic-themed units in the National Park System, advanced the cause of women hires and getting women into leadership positions, and diversified our nation's stories during the commemoration of significant national events such as the Sesquicentennial of the Civil War, 400 years of slavery, and the 19th Amendment.

Through the internet and other technological advancements, the NPS has been able to reach and engage wider and more diverse audiences, especially within schools around the country. National park interpreters, education specialists, and public affairs staff have also been able to bring the national parks and their stories directly to students through onsite visits, web broadcasts, and other technologies.

NPS youth programs have helped to prepare and provide paid experiences for those interested in becoming a museum curator or a park ranger. With a commitment to diversity, youth and young adults ages up to age thirty, and veterans thirty-five years old or younger, are invited to discover opportunities in national parks. Agency internships also provide an additional opportunity to acquire hands-on work experience.

Created in 2011 at Grand Teton National Park, the NPS Academy is also promoting and building the next NPS workforce, as well as conservation stewards and advocates with an emphasis on diversity. Each year, the program includes separate phases to assist academy members along their path toward a possible career with the National Park Service.

After the spring break phase of the program, the college students are placed in internships in national park sites around the U.S. with many of them returning to Grand Teton. The students spend their summers working in various offices from interpretation and visitor services, vegetation management, to social sciences to name a few.

One of the most significant developments in the 102-year history of the National Park Service was the development of the Workforce, Relevancy, and Inclusion Directorate located in NPS Headquarters in Washington, DC. For the first time in the agency's history, an entire directorate located in the director's corridor would promote, advance, and leverage capacity at a national level for RDI. I was honored to have been appointed as the first associate director for this new directorate by Director Jarvis and Deputy Director Peggy O'dell.

In addition to what the NPS was achieving on the youth and diversity front, I enjoyed tremendously the opportunity to work with and to better understand the growing number of nonprofit organizations that have been created to help engage and promote outdoor experiences and resource protection within communities of color throughout the country. Mark

Magaña, the founding President and CEO of GreenLatinos, is one such example.

As a national network of Latino environmental and conservation advocates, GreenLatinos brings together a broad coalition of Latino leaders who are committed to addressing environmental and conservation issues that significantly affect the health and welfare of the U.S. Latino community across the nation. Diverse organizations such as GreenLatinos also play an extremely important role in assisting the NPS and the conservation community in building the next generation of conservation stewards, advocates, and members of the workforce.

Another important organization is the National History Academy, which was developed to inspire students and promote a better understanding of the foundations of American democracy and citizenship through experiential learning. With a commitment to diversity, and through the interaction with fellow students in historic places, the Academy develops analytical thinking skills as they evaluate difficult moments in American history while relating those moments to issues that we face today.

I have been extremely fortunate to have risen through the ranks in the National Park Service and, as a senior executive, run complex organizations as a superintendent, regional director, associate director, deputy director, and acting director. Within these roles, and with the support of my staff, we were able to help promote and pursue workforce diversity as well as find ways to effectively engage communities of color while promoting their stories as part of our nation's history.

I learned that one of the principal challenges for the National Park Service has been failing to make the business case for RDI at every level of our organization, not sustaining park and national diversity initiatives that work, and in not fully embracing RDI as part of our organizational culture. Federal agencies can have robust RDI programs and initiatives but if it is not fully embodied in its organizational architecture and DNA, "the house will not stand."

We will have a unique opportunity to better understand each other and our collective history in July 2026 as the nation commemorates the 250th anniversary of our founding. The commemoration provides an unparalleled opportunity to celebrate the democratic values enshrined in the Declaration of Independence, to explore who and how people of color helped to build and fight for the ideals that guide us as a country and the lessons that we have learned to date.

Through dialogue and workshops with diverse affinity groups within the NPS, a roadmap was developed to help ensure that all of America connects to this historic occasion in an inclusive and meaningful way.

From acknowledging the true origins and history of the United States to having every park visitor who interacts with NPS parks and programs see themselves in our nation's collective story, I am so very proud of how the National Park Service is taking a leading role in this milestone event in American history.

With recent racial and social unrest around the country, the NPS is uniquely positioned to share the lessons learned from the historic battlefields, monuments and memorials, and stories and programs that it manages. This history not only provides opportunities for reflection, it also enables us to assess the lessons of the past and their relevance to our nation today. Most importantly, we learn from history that we cannot take our democratic and constitutional values for granted.

Through my business travels, I would meet NPS employees around the country and would immediately get a very favorable impression. It's like you knew that the employee would rise through the organization as a result of their professionalism, demeanor, and humility. Pamela A. Smith of the United States Park Police is one such individual.

A twenty-three-year veteran of the USPP, Pam would become the first African American woman to lead the 230-year-old agency. I had the opportunity to meet the chief when she was the commander of the New York field office. As chief, she proudly leads a 560-member workforce that protects our most iconic landmarks in our nation's capital, New York City, and San Francisco. Congratulations, my dear friend—I am so very proud of your accomplishments!

Creating and sustaining a relevant, diverse, and inclusive culture and organization will help to connect with and create the next generation of park visitors, supporters, and advocates. In addition, it will help to heal our great nation while helping to create a more perfect Union.

CHAPTER 22

EPILOGUE

Hola Ranger is not a history of the National Park Service, nor does it contain major policy or regulatory outcomes as there are publications that have already been written (and those that will follow) that will address these important concerns.

This is a book that provides a roadmap for how a Latino country boy from Southeast Texas realized his dream. In addition, it honors the achievements and sacrifices of all NPS employees as well as colleagues of color who made their journey through the national parks and opened the door for my own journey.

Whether they realized it or not, their work over many decades helped to open doors of opportunity for future generations in the National Park Service. In addition, they also demonstrated that Latinos and people of color can play a vital role within the NPS workforce in telling our nation's stories and in protecting the many treasures found within our National Park System.

Although I may be a little biased, I wholeheartedly agree with writer and historian Wallace Stegner who called our national parks "the best idea we ever had. Absolutely

American, absolutely democratic, they reflect us at our best rather than our worst."

Since their creation, units of the National Park Service have provided comfort and insight during difficult times as well as opportunities to recreate and experience some of the most majestic places on the face of the earth. We need them as they need us for the protection and enjoyment of current generations and those to come.

So, I have a special message for our nation's youth. If you decide that you want to take on a cause greater than yourself and protect some of our nation's most special places as a National Park Service employee—stay the course! Do not be discouraged by all of the administrative processes that are involved as well as the time that it may take.

Be patient and do all that you can to make yourself marketable. Remember, the life decisions you make today may impact your future employment prospects. Therefore, always maintain a strong moral and ethical compass. In the end, it is worth the effort, and the rewards will last a lifetime.

If you are interested in a career in the National Park Service, what we do may not be well known to families of color as they may have never visited and or experienced a national park. Explain why, and how they may also have the opportunity to share in your journey and experiences— whether in a park or program office—and take your family and friends to the national parks.

Take, for example, the story of my cousin, Alejandra (Ale) Briseno: "The summer before my last year of high school, I did not know who I wanted to be. I heard about the Youth Conservation Program from David Vela. I never imagined myself working in a National Park, but I didn't hesitate to submit my application. Weeks later, I found myself in the middle of the Teton mountain range fighting to protect the environment. Working in the National Park included rigorous manual labor, learning about the surrounding flora and fauna, and hearing about the rich history of the land and surviving historic sites."

In addition, Ale stated, "Going back home to complete my senior year, I had finally discovered my calling. I knew I needed to advocate for the conservation of the environment. I had the overall concept I wanted to follow, but it took a few semesters in college to determine how I wanted to protect the environment. I chose to pursue a scientific route in the field of geosciences. Studying geology has allowed me to spend time learning about the earth. I am

Alejandra Briseno, Grand Teton National Park, 2015, Texas A&M University Graduate 2020, Briseno Family Photo

currently analyzing the water quality of a lagoon in Texas. Although I am barely beginning my journey, I look forward to where my future will take me. I will always be an active environmentalist spreading the word about how we should be better at caring for our planet—and that all began when I stepped foot into a National Park."

As with Ale's journey, one experience and one opportunity can potentially change your entire perspective on life. Going beyond your comfort zone and experiencing your national heritage in our national parks may provide the same life-changing experience—as it did for me.

Through our son Anthony and daughter-in-law Amelia Vela, a second generation is now navigating their own journey as employees of the National Park Service. It is my hope that their generation, and those that follow, will carry on the proud traditions of conservation stewardship and the values that have made the National Park Service one of our nation's most beloved agencies.

Anthony and Amelia Vela, 2018
Vela Family Photo

Author and son Anthony
Vela Family Photo

To all of my fellow grand-parents, it is my hope that you will join me in opening up a world of exploration in our national parks for your families, whether walking down the historic cobble-stone streets of Independence National Historical Park or floating down the Snake River in Grand Teton National Park. As with my parents, all you

Nathaniel Anthony Vela, 2018
Vela Family Photo

need is a desire for exploration, a bag of corn chips, and a loaf of bread. Who knows? Maybe we will run into each other on your journey.

During the course of my years of public service, I would hear from time to time the comment, "Your legacy can be defined by ..." or, "if you do not achieve this, it will affect your legacy ..." My response was always the same: whatever legacy or footprint I have left on the landscape will never be defined by what I did in the workplace but what I did on the home front.

In other words, having had the honor of wearing the "green and gray," my over forty years of marriage with my high school sweetheart, my family, and a deep and abiding faith and love of country will forever define me.

In the end, it is my hope that my grandfather, a share-cropper, is looking down on me with a smile for a job well done! So, may your own experiences and journey through our national parks be as rewarding and memorable as mine.

Author's Grandchildren
(L/R) Gabriel, Issaac, Noah, Mariah, Nathaniel, Xavier
Vela Family Photo

Kingston Ray Vela,
7th Grandchild, 2021
Vela Family Photo

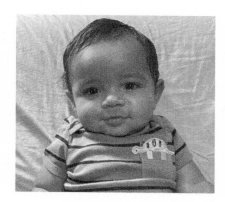

APPENDIX A

ACKNOWLEDGEMENTS

O ne of my greatest joys as a National Park Service employee was to learn about, know directly, or work with those who administered the National Park Service. They included:

Ronald H. Walker, January 7, 1973 to January 3, 1975

President Richard Nixon appointed Ronald H. Walker, an advance man on his staff, as the eighth director of the National Park Service. Director Walker brought fourteen areas into the park system during his two years as director, including the first two national preserves. His wife Anne chronicled his advance work for the President in China in a book entitled *China Calls, Paving the Way for Nixon's Historic Journey to China*. As a seasonal resident of Jackson Hole, I had the benefit of their wisdom, experiences, and friendship while I served as Grand Teton National Park superintendent, as acting director in Washington, DC, and now in retirement.

Gary Everhardt, January 13, 1975 to May 27, 1977

Gary Everhardt began his NPS career as an engineer in 1957 and rose through the ranks to become the superintendent of Grand Teton National Park in 1972. His efforts gained favorable notice, which propelled him to become the ninth director in January 1975. As director, he oversaw a great increase in park development and interpretive programming for the bicentennial of the American Revolution. Under the Carter Administration, he returned to the field as the superintendent of the Blue Ridge Parkway in May 1977. Gary died in 2020.

Russell E. Dickenson, May 15, 1980 to March 3, 1985

Russell E. Dickenson rose through the ranks of the National Park Service to become the eleventh director, and was the only Department bureau chief to be retained by the Reagan Administration in 1981. He was also the first director who I would meet while serving as a cooperative education student and rookie national park ranger. Director Dickenson retired in March 1985 and died in 2008.

Robert Stanton, August 4, 1997 to January 2001

Beginning his National Park Service career as a seasonal ranger at Grand Teton National Park in 1962, director Stanton was another example of a career employee who rose through the ranks before retiring in January 1997. However, in August of that year, the Clinton Administration brought him back home, and in the process, he became our first African American director. His legacy includes increasing the diversity of the service's staff and public programs to better serve minority populations around the country. He also assisted in bringing me back home to the service in 1998 and remains one of my very valued friends and mentors.

Fran P. Mainella, July 18, 2001 to October 16, 2006

Fran P. Mainella was nominated by President Bush and became the sixteenth director of the National Park Service as well as the first woman to administer the agency. Director Mainella brought to the job over thirty years of experience in the park management and recreation field. She would also be the first director to provide me with a front row seat while in a detail assignment in her office to experience the challenges and opportunities of administering the National Park Service. I continue to seek and greatly value her continued guidance and friendship.

Mary Bomar, October 17, 2006 to January 20, 2009

Upon confirmation by the U.S. Senate, Mary A. Bomar became the seventeenth director of the National Park Service as well as the first naturalized citizen to lead the agency. However, many years prior to this appointment, we were rookie park superintendents and colleagues together in the Intermountain Region of the National Park Service. I will always be grateful for her confidence and support of my entry into the Senior Executive Service as a regional director, and for her continued friendship.

Jon Jarvis, October 2, 2009 to January 3, 2017

As an employee holding many career as well as leadership positions within the agency, Jonathan B. Jarvis was sworn in as the eighteenth director of the National Park Service by

Interior Secretary Ken Salazar. We would first know and work together in our capacity as regional directors. His institutional knowledge, passion for the mission of the agency, and friendship is greatly valued and appreciated.

APPENDIX B

NOTES

Chapter 1

The legislative mandate of the National Park Service is simple and yet complex: "... to conserve the scenery and the natural and historic objects and the wildlife therein and to provide for the enjoyment of the same in such manner and by such means as will leave them unimpaired for the enjoyment of future generations."

George Melendez Wright was born in San Francisco, California, to a Salvadoran mother on June 20, 1904, and his interest in science was promoted by a great aunt who cared for him after the death of his parents when he was a child. He enrolled at the University of California, Berkeley, to study forestry and vertebrate zoology. George joined the staff of Yosemite National Park as an assistant park naturalist in 1927 and left a lasting legacy in helping to achieve the mission of the National Park Service.

Chapter 2

A plantation community was settled in 1846 along the Colorado River by some of Stephen F. Austin's original colonists. The following year, a post office was established in 1847. European Jewish immigrants began arriving in the community as early as the 1850s from Germany as well as other settlers including Mexican, German, Swiss, and Czech immigrants and descendants of plantation slaves after the Civil War and emancipation. The city was primarily developed for agriculture.

Planters used enslaved African Americans for labor prior to the Civil War. Potatoes, cotton, corn, rice, and cattle helped to fuel the economy and commercial interests, as did the extraction of sulfur and oil in the surrounding area. The New York, Texas, and Mexican Railway was the first railroad to reach Wharton in 1881.

Most of the buildings in Wharton in 1902 were constructed of wood when it was incorporated. A major fire on December 30, 1902, destroyed a number of frame business buildings. Afterward, businessmen and the city government were convinced to use brick construction with fire walls for all buildings within the city limits and to construct a water system with fire hydrants. A free library was established in 1902, and the first public park was dedicated in 1913. Wharton County Junior College was established in 1946.

In 1960, the town's population reached 5,734 and 7,881 in 1970. The population of Wharton was relatively stable by the end of the 20th century with 9,033 in 1980, 9,011 in 1990, and 9,237 in 2000. The 2010 census reported a decrease to 8,832.

Chapter 3

Over the decades, the National Park Service uniform underwent several major changes, although the "flat hat" remains a direct link back to the nineteenth century. The uniform eventually settled on the gray shirt and green trousers that can be seen on NPS rangers today.

With the exception of NPS law enforcement rangers and United States Park Police officers, the badge is a gold shield embossed with "National Park Ranger" and the seal of the U.S. Department of the Interior dated March 3, 1849 (when the Department was established). In addition, standing on grass in the middle of the shield, a bison is facing to the left with a background of mountains and a rising sun.

Recognized by visitors from around the world, the NPS arrowhead was authorized as the official National Park Service emblem by the Secretary of the Interior on July 20, 1951. The arrowhead emblem symbolizes the major components of the national park system. The Sequoia tree and bison represent vegetation and wildlife, the mountains and water represent scenic and recreational values, and the arrowhead represents historical and archeological values.

Chapter 4

Denied a decent and safe existence in the agricultural fields of California, César Chávez founded the National Farm Workers Association in 1962 later to become the United Farm Workers. He believed that for every violent act committed against Latinos, a nonviolent response was necessary in order to attract widespread support. He also believed that the American people would respond more positively to nonviolent actions and to their ongoing struggle to achieve the American dream. César Chávez died on April 23, 1993, near Yuma, Arizona.

Chapter 5

Wharton County Junior College's production of the *Wizard of Oz* was an exhilarating yet demanding production. From set design and construction to the performance of all of the actors, it was the experience of a lifetime. However, the fumes from the silver-colored face paint caused migraine headaches after each performance. The role of the "scarecrow" was played by my wife's cousin, Abel Suaste (now deceased).

Author, 1979, Vela Family Photo

Chapter 6

The Medal of Honor citation for Roy Benavidez reflected upon his extremely valorous actions in the face of overwhelming odds and reads as follows: "The President of the United States of America, authorized by act of Congress, March 3, 1863, has awarded in the name of the Congress the Medal of Honor to Master Sergeant Roy P. Benavidez, United States Army (Retired), for conspicuous gallantry and intrepidity in action at the risk of his life above and beyond the call of duty.

On the morning of 2 May 1968, a 12-man Special Forces Reconnaissance Team was inserted by helicopters of the 240th Assault Helicopter Company in a dense jungle area west of Loc Ninh, Vietnam to gather intelligence information about confirmed large-scale enemy activity. The area was controlled and routinely patrolled by the North Vietnamese Army. After a short period of time on the ground, the

The author with Roy and his wife Lala for the baptism of Anthony, 1988, Vela Family Photo

team met heavy enemy resistance, and requested emergency extraction. Three helicopters attempted extraction, but were unable to land due to intense enemy small arms and anti-aircraft fire. Sergeant Benavidez was at the Forward Operating Base in Loc Ninh monitoring the operation by radio when these helicopters, of the 240th Assault Helicopter Company, returned to off-load wounded crew members and to assess aircraft damage. Sergeant Benavidez voluntarily boarded a returning aircraft to assist in another extraction attempt. Realizing that all the team members were either dead or wounded and unable to move to the pickup zone, he directed the aircraft to a nearby clearing where he jumped from the hovering helicopter, and ran approximately 75 meters under withering small arms fired to the crippled team. Prior to reaching the team's position, he was wounded in his right leg, face, and head. Despite these painful injuries, he took charge, repositioning the team members and directing their fire to facilitate the landing of an extraction aircraft, and the loading of wounded and dead team members. He then threw smoke canisters to direct the aircraft to the team's position. Despite his severe wounds and under intense enemy fire, he carried and dragged half of the wounded team members to the awaiting aircraft. He then provided protective fire by running alongside the aircraft as it moved to pick up the remaining team members. As the enemy's fire intensified, he hurried to recover the body and classified documents on the dead team leader. When he reached the leader's body, Sergeant Benavidez was severely wound by small arms fire in the abdomen and grenade fragments in his back. At nearly the same moment, the aircraft pilot was mortally wounded, and his helicopter crashed. Although in extremely critical condition due to his multiple wounds, Sergeant Benavidez secured the classified documents and made his way back to the wreckage, where he aided the wounded out of the overturned aircraft, and gathered the stunned survivors into a defensive perimeter. Under increasing enemy automatic weapons and grenade fire, he moved around the perimeter distributing water and ammunition to his weary men, reinstilling in them a will to live and fight. Facing a buildup of enemy opposition with a beleaguered team, Sergeant Benavidez mustered his strength, began calling in tactical air strikes, and directed the fire from supporting gunships to suppress the enemy's fire and so permit another extraction attempt. He was wounded again in his thigh by small arms fire while administering first aid to a wounded team member just before another extraction helicopter was able to land. His indomitable spirit kept him going as he began to ferry his comrades to the craft. On his second trip with the wounded, he was clubbed from behind by an enemy soldier. In the ensuing hand-to-hand combat, he sustained additional wounds to his head and arms before killing his adversary. He then continued under devastating fire to carry the wounded to the helicopter. Upon reaching the aircraft, he spotted and killed two enemy soldiers who were rushing the craft from an angle that prevented the aircraft door gunner from firing upon them. With little strength remaining, he made one last trip to the perimeter to ensure that all classified material had been collected or destroyed, and to bring in the wounded. Only then, in extremely serious condition from numerous wounds and loss of blood did he allow himself to be pulled into the extraction aircraft. Sergeant Benavidez's gallant choice to join voluntarily his comrades who were in serious straits, to expose himself to constant withering fire, and his refusal to stop despite numerous severe wounds, saved the lives of at least eight men. His fearless personal leadership, tenacious devotion to duty, and extremely valorous actions in the face of overwhelming odds, were in keeping with the highest traditions of the military service, and reflect the upmost credit on him and the United States Army."

Chapter 7

Opening its doors in 1876 as the state's first public institution of higher learning, Texas A&M University offers 133 undergraduate degree programs, 175 master's degree programs, ninety-two doctoral degree programs, and five first professional degrees. As a research-intensive university, it is preparing the next generation of leaders to take on the challenges of tomorrow.

The Recreation, Park, and Tourism Sciences Department at Texas A&M University is consistently ranked among the top three programs in the country and among the top ten programs in the world in tourism. Over the decades, the Department produced many graduates who became park rangers and park professionals at all levels of government, to include me. Under the leadership of Dr. Scott Shafer, department head and professor and his amazing team, they will continue to inspire and attract the next generation with an emphasis on reaching diverse communities.

In his memoirs, *The Making of a Ranger: Forty Years with the National Parks*, Lon stated, "Other rangers with equal zeal have extended the horizon here and elsewhere. Later generations must decide if we did it well. At least the treasures remain about which to make decisions! Our vote is in—a ranger career was a great way to go!"

De Soto National Memorial was established in 1948 to commemorate the 1539 expedition of Spanish Conquistador Hernando de Soto and his impact on the American Indian communities of the Southeast. One of the primary features of the park is Camp Uzita, which was constructed to resemble De Soto's base camp at the Indian village of Uzita.

Under Captain Pedro Calderon's command, approximately one hundred soldiers, sailors, and horseman operated the camp as a supply port. With instructions provided by De Soto, they were to remain in place until he sent them new orders. For five months, Calderon's company guarded the expedition's supplies while De Soto and the main army marched north toward what is now Tallahassee, Florida. De Soto ordered Captain Calderon to abandon the base camp in order to join the main army for the winter of 1539.

I will always be grateful to Farrell Saunders (now retired) who was my first supervisor and who also served as a superintendent later in his career as well as (retired) De Soto Superintendent Dick Hite. Both have been dear friends all these many years.

Chapter 8

Along with native hunters and gathers, Spanish explorers were attracted to the lush area surrounding the San Antonio River. The missions flourished between 1745 and the 1780s. However, increasing hostility from the Apache and later the Comanche, in addition to inadequate military support, caused the communities to retreat behind the walls of the mission compound. In addition, disease reduced the native population and accelerated the missions' decline.

There are several gateways that provide entrance into the compounds of the walled Spanish mission communities. Bastions, or fortified towers, were located along the walls to provide defensive support while the living quarters were built inside and against the compound walls. The focal point of the mission community was the church. The convent, workshops, and storage rooms were located within the compound grounds while ranching and agricultural activities were located outside of the mission walls.

The United Nations Educational, Scientific, and Cultural Organization (UNESCO), designated San Antonio's five Spanish colonial missions as a World Heritage Site. Known for their extremely exceptional cultural and natural properties,

San Antonio Missions National Historical Park and the Alamo were designated as a UNESCO World Heritage Site on July 5, 2015.

Libby Hulett's husband, B.C. "Barney" Hulett, was an Army presidential helicopter pilot from 1959 to 1967 and was with the elite helicopter unit that supported the White House. He was present during three administrations and also flew for the L.B.J. Company. Barney is the author of *Twenty Bosses*, which relates his experience of twenty-one years of military life and twenty-one years of flying for the L.B.J. Company.

Stephen Mather, the first director of the National Park Service, once said, "If a trail is to be blazed, send a ranger, if an animal is floundering in the snow, send a ranger, if a bear is in a hotel, send a ranger, if a fire threatens a forest, send a ranger, and if someone needs to be saved, send a ranger." I would now begin my journey as a national park ranger, and would have the opportunity to meet my first NPS director—Russell E. Dickenson, eleventh director of the National Park Service. Since our Grand Canyon experience at The Horace M. Albright Training Center, I have had a number of colleagues who have since retired and a couple who are still wearing the "green and gray." To Marta Cruz Kelly, Mike Grant, Patti Reilly, Eric Williams, Ron Crayton, Larry Johnson, and Fred Armstrong who were my hiking and field training buddies, thanks for your lasting friendship and service in protecting our nation's most special places.

There were many wonderful memories of my first permanent NPS assignment in San Antonio, including the birth of our first child, Christina Yvonne Vela. Christina was born on February 11, 1984, and was baptized at Mission San Juan by Victor and Lupe Carrasco. Victor was the park's chief ranger. Prior to leaving for our next assignment, I served as the site supervisor for Mission San Jose, the park's largest mission unit.

Chapter 9

George Peers served as the Appomattox County Clerk during the time of the surrender. An original structure that was constructed in 1855, the Peers House was located on a rise overlooking the village of Appomattox Court House and was an eyewitness to history when General Lee surrendered to General Grant. The structure is consistent in style and development of a mid-nineteenth century rural Virginia home.

Confederate soldiers would walk past the Peers House, which was located on the Richmond-Lynchburg Stage Road, to

The Peers House, Appomattox Court
House National Historical Park, 1985,
Vela Family Photo

go into battle on April 9, 1865, and they would later lay down their arms there on April 12, 1865. On the morning of April 9, 1865, one of the final artillery shots fired by Confederate forces would kill Lieutenant Hiram Clark of the 185th New York Infantry near the Peers House.

An employee and close friend of over thirty-five years, Gerry Gaumer, who lived in government quarters near the village, would later occupy my position and live in the Peers House. I was extremely fortunate to have a very knowledgeable and capable staff as well as park volunteers. Gerry was one of the best in the performance of his duties, and in serving as a living history reenactor.

There is a practice in the National Park Service that is exercised around every two to four years—the move. Normally, a promotion is involved, or there is a desire to pursue a different park, training, or program experience. It is also possible for an employee to spend their entire career in one park or program office as it is ultimately the employee's decision. On the other hand, there are some hiring officials who value seeing a diversity of work experiences around the NPS with varying degrees of complexity when making hiring decisions.

Chapter 10

Located in historic downtown Philadelphia, Independence National Historical Park is often referred to as the birthplace of our nation. Visitors can experience the Liberty Bell and Independence Hall, a World Heritage Site, where both the Declaration of Independence and the U.S. Constitution were created. In addition, the park reveals the lives and events of a diverse population during the years when Philadelphia was the capital of the United States from 1790 to 1800. It is where Benjamin Franklin's home once stood, and where Franklin's life and accomplishments unfolded.

The Inspector General Act of 1978 created twelve departmental inspectors general (IGs). In October 2008, the Inspector General Reform Act of 2008 added IGs in various other areas. Special agents (criminal investigators, often armed) and auditors are employed to detect and prevent fraud, waste, abuse, and mismanagement of government programs and operations. Investigations may be internal, targeting government employees, or external, targeting recipients of federal domestic and foreign assistance programs.

Chapter 11

George Thomas "Mickey" Leland was born on November 27, 1944. Mickey was a strong and effective advocate for hunger and public health issues among other social interests.

Representing the 88th District, Mickey served three two-year terms in the Texas House of Representatives. He was renowned for his staunch advocacy of healthcare rights for the poor in Texas. In November 1978, he was elected to represent the 18th Congressional District of Texas and was re-elected to six two-year terms.

As an African American member of Congress, he was recognized for his commitment to health, children, and the elderly. In 1984, he established the Congressional Select Committee on Hunger and initiated a number of programs designed to address the dire needs of famine that was plaguing Ethiopia and Sudan.

Chapter 12

The attorney general of Texas serves as the chief legal officer as provided by the Texas Constitution and statutes. Some of the main responsibilities of the Office of Attorney General include defending the State of Texas; providing legal representation and rendering legal opinions; enforcement of the state's child support laws and the collection of child support: investigating and prosecuting criminal activities; assisting local law enforcement in prosecutions and appeals; and providing support to victims of violent crime and administering victim assistance programs.

Born on April 24, 1956, Daniel C. Morales served as the forty-eighth attorney general of Texas from January 15, 1991 through January 13, 1999. Following his graduation from Harvard Law School, Dan worked for a corporate law firm, and in 1981, he joined the Bexar County district attorney's office. At twenty-eight years of age, he ran successfully for the Texas House of Representatives, representing the 124th District of San Antonio, and was re-elected in 1986 and 1988.

Attorney General Dan Morales with the author's son Anthony, 1991, Vela Family Photo

After six years in the legislature, Dan announced and won his candidacy for attorney general of Texas, and was reelected to a second term. He joined other states in filing a federal lawsuit accusing the tobacco industry of racketeering and fraud and sought reimbursement of health care costs related to smoking. The Texas state treasury received millions of dollars from the litigation.

However, Dan later admitted to having falsified documents in an attempt to give another lawyer a portion of the state's tobacco settlement. On October 2003, he reached a plea agreement and served time in the Federal Correctional Institution in Texarkana, Texas, and was released to a halfway house near San Antonio in 2006.

Although we have not spoken to the former attorney general in over twenty years, Melissa and I will always be grateful for the opportunity that he gave us to serve the people of Texas, and for his friendship.

Chapter 13

On May 8, 1846, American and Mexican troops clashed on the prairie of Palo Alto in the first battle of a war lasting two years. Authorized by Congress in 1978 as Palo Alto Battlefield National Historic Site (now a National Historical Park) preserves the 3,400-acre scene of this clash between nations and informs visitors about its national and international importance.

Following the Mexican defeat at the Battle of Palo Alto the previous day, Mexican General Mariano Arista moved his forces to a more defensible position along a resaca known as Resaca de Guerrero or Resaca de la Palma. The dense brush offered his troops plenty of protective cover as they hoped to force an infantry battle in the dense chaparral instead of the open-field artillery duel that had devastated them at Palo Alto.

Resaca de la Palma was one of many long, water-filled ravines left behind by the shifting course of the Rio Grande river. Lined with dense brush dotted with pools of water, the Mexican Army hoped that these natural features would limit any attack against their troops.

General Zachary Taylor followed Arista's force from Palo Alto to the old resaca. As U.S. artillery fired on Mexican batteries guarding the resaca crossing, they engaged Mexican soldiers in furious hand-to-hand combat. The victory at Resaca de la Palma ended the six-day siege of Fort Texas and left the north bank of the lower Rio Grande firmly in the grasp of United States forces. The battle at Resaca de la Palma inspired the confidence of the American soldiers.

With the dedicated support of my staff, private citizens such as Frank and Mary Yturria and Walter and Molly Plitt, community organizations to include the Brownsville Community Foundation, Cameron County commissioners (Commissioner John Wood in particular), and officials appointed by Mayor Blanca Vela (Larry Brown, Brownsville Airport Director and Police Chief Ben Reyna) as well as our

(L/R) Palo Alto Battlefield National Historic Site staff—
Rolando Garza, Karen Weaver, Carol Gonzalez, Luis Krug,
Oralia Fernandez, Doug Murphy, and the author, 2002,
NPS Photo

Congressional delegation, funds were raised and facilities were built on the battlefield.

John Nau's lifelong interest and passion for American history has served him and the nation well while serving as chairman of the Advisory Council on Historic Preservation, which is appointed by the President of the United States. He also served and is currently serving as chairman of the Texas Historical Commission, which is an appointed position by the governor of Texas. While in Brownsville, and for over twenty years, I have greatly valued his sage advice, guidance, counsel and, most importantly, his friendship.

Chapter 14

Lyndon B. Johnson National Historical Park tells the story of our thirty-sixth President. Authorized on December 2, 1969, it was redesignated from a historic site to a national historical park on December 28, 1980.

The story begins with Lyndon Johnson's ancestors, tracing the influences his family and his beloved Texas Hill Country had on the boy and the man. In 1909, the President's aunt and uncle, Frank and Clarence Martin, bought the house and added the central portion of the home. The Johnsons bought the home from his aunt in 1951. Needing considerable work, they made a number of additions to include the master bedrooms and the office wing.

The gem of the famed LBJ Ranch, the home of President Johnson, was a center of political activity for more than twenty years. Leaders from around the world visited the Johnsons, and during his administration it became known as the Texas White House. The original section of the house was constructed of native limestone in 1894.

Chapter 15

The George Washington Memorial Parkway preserves the natural scenery along the Potomac River and connects the historic sites from Mount Vernon, where Washington lived, past the nation's capital, which he founded, and to the Great Falls of the Potomac where the President demonstrated his skills as an engineer.

Developed as a memorial to George Washington, the parkway is used as a scenic corridor to travel to historical, natural, and recreational areas. These places are all linked by this planned and landscaped road, the first section of which was completed in 1932 to commemorate the bicentennial of George Washington's birth. It also protects the Potomac River shoreline and watershed, and passes through the same lands where George Washington frequently traveled by horse.

Chapter 16

As I write *Hola Ranger*, Melissa and I have celebrated over forty years of marriage. Our closeness has meant that being away from home for extended periods of time whether for training and detail assignments was always difficult. This reminds me of when I had to explain to Melissa's parents why we needed to move from San Antonio, Texas, to Appomattox, Virginia. However, the detail assignment as acting deputy regional director, and time away from home, would provide a return on investment.

Equivalent to general officer or flag officer ranks in the U.S. Armed Forces, the Senior Executive Service (SES) was created in 1979 when the Civil Service Reform Act of 1978 went into effect under President Jimmy Carter. With a membership selected for their leadership qualifications, the SES was designed to be a corps of federal executives serving below presidential appointees as a link to the rest of the federal civil service workforce. I would become a member of the SES corps in 2008 as a regional director.

The Southeast Region includes three of the top ten most visited attractions in the National Park System and welcomes approximately one-fourth of all visitors to America's national parks. As regional director, I was providing support for sixty-six park units located throughout nine states, the U.S. Virgin Islands, and Puerto Rico.

In the NPS publication, "Slavery: Cause and Catalyst of the Civil War," the question is raised, "What caused the Civil War? A number of issues ignited the Civil War: states' rights, the role of the federal government, the preservation of the Union, the economy, but all were inextricably bound to the institution of slavery."

The NPS publication, "Hispanics and the Civil War: From Battlefield to Homefront" provides a glimpse into some of the lives, stories, and achievements of Hispanics who fought and struggled for a more perfect Union. From the opening shots at Fort Sumter, South Carolina, to the final actions at Palmito Ranch near Brownsville, Texas, in 1865, many Hispanics chose to fight for the cause of the Union and Confederacy for a variety of reasons.

The publication also describes descendants of Spanish explorers and settlers making homes along the bayous, on large plantations, and in the port cities of the Gulf Coast. Hispanic soldiers fought at Antietam, Gettysburg, Vicksburg, and in other epic battles. It ends by stating, "Hispanics were very much a part of this conflict. They knew hardship, fear, death, and destruction. They experienced victory and defeat. Some performed acts of spectacular gallantry. Others provided steady service that attracted little comment or notice. All merit recognition, not just for the honor they brought upon the Hispanic American community, but for their service and sacrifice as Americans in the nation's greatest struggle— the Civil War."

Through the collective efforts of Donald (Don) Wollenhaupt, chief of interpretation and education (now retired) for the Southeast Region, Carol Shively, communications coordinator for the Civil War to Civil Rights Commemoration for the Southeast Regional Office, and our team, communities of color may have for the first time found relevancy as well as a better understanding of the actions of their ancestors during one of the most trying times in our nation's history.

Secretary of the Interior Ken Salazar encouraged the National Park Service to consider how American Latino heritage could be better integrated into the story of America. On June 16, 2011, the Department, NPS, and the National Park Foundation hosted "The La Paz Forum," a day-long event held at the National Chavez Center at La Paz in Keene, California. La Paz served as the headquarters and refuge for Chavez in his efforts to organize poor people and disenfranchised farm workers.

Utilizing the knowledge shared at the Forum, the National Park Service agreed to perform the following: initiate an American Latino Theme Study, recommend potential designations significant to Latino heritage as national historic landmarks, expand the interpretation at existing Latino Heritage sites, and develop new funding to aid in the establishment of new national park sites and national historic landmarks.

The St. Augustine 450th anniversary provided a compelling case study of American history. From its beginnings, it contained a tremendous mixture of people from the Timucua, Spanish, British, and American settlements. American Indians from the Southern Plains were imprisoned within the fort in the 1870s. Martin Luther King, Jr. helped to focus the nation's attention on St. Augustine's segregation during the spring of 1964 as Congress debated the Civil Rights Act.

Castillo de San Marcos and Fort Matanzas National Monument's superintendent Gordon "Gordie" Wilson and his amazing staff continue to do an excellent job in ensuring that this complex case study in American history is told as it will always remain an important and ongoing part of our nation's narrative and of the Latino community.

Castillo de San Marcos National Monument, 2021, Vela Family Photo

A bison on the Grand Teton Range, 2018,
Vela Family Photo

Chapter 17

I must admit I was in awe and a little intimidated by this isolated Western landscape but soon gained more confidence as each day passed that we could not only live but thrive in this unfamiliar environment. Then there was the wildlife— an American Serengeti— that had free-roaming bison, elk, moose, grizzly and black bears, and pronghorn. Plus, there are opportunities for world-class fly fishing, floating the Snake River, and backcountry hiking. Grand Teton National Park offers a world of exploration and memorable experiences.

The park also has a fascinating human footprint, including American Indians, fur trappers, surveyors, homesteaders, dude ranches, and a rich array of historic cabins. We completed a Historic Properties Management Plan/Environmental Assessment that evaluates present conditions and future uses for the forty-four historic properties located within Grand Teton National Park and the John D. Rockefeller Jr. Memorial Parkway.

Growing up on the Triangle X Ranch with his brothers Harold and Donald, John Turner had a prestigious career in public service that encompassed serving as a Wyoming state representative and senator, director of the United States Fish and Wildlife Service under President George W. Bush's Administration, and serving as assistant secretary of state for oceans and international environmental and scientific affairs.

Mary Kay Turner has a life-long passion for and achievements in addressing literacy, education, and the needs for families and women around the world.

One of my predecessors, former Grand Teton National Park Superintendent Jack Neckels, along with my dear friend the late Jerry Halpin, gathered a small group of people together in 1997 to discuss the prospect of having a visitor center for the park. With that vision in mind, and with their founding board of directors, they set out to raise funds for a state-of-the art visitor center. This successful project set the stage for the Foundation to gift millions of dollars to the park each year through the support of generous donors and partners.

On December 12, 2016, the National Park Service purchased 640 acres in Grand Teton National Park from the State of Wyoming. A special and heartfelt thanks to former Secretary of the Interior Sally Jewell; former NPS Director Jon Jarvis; Leslie Mattson, President, Grand Teton National Park Foundation; and Will Shafroth, President and CEO of the National Park Foundation for their leadership and support in helping to make this acquisition a reality. In addition, thanks as well to my dear friend and former colleague, Gary Pollock (senior advisor to the superintendent). The children of Wyoming were also an important benefactor, as the proceeds of the $46 million dollar sale will benefit public school students.

In addition to inspiring the next generation of park stewards, the National Park Foundation helps to protect America's special places while connecting people to our national heritage. The National Park Foundation is also the official nonprofit partner of the National Park Service. President and CEO Will Shafroth leads the organization's work to inspire all people to connect with and protect America's national parks.

Another valued partner who advocated for the protection of the park's outstanding natural and cultural resources was the National Parks Conservation Association (NPCA). We worked collaboratively with Sharon Mader, senior program manager for the Northern Rockies Region, to find creative and innovative funding and legislative solutions to permanently protect threatened lands in Grand Teton National Park.

It soon became clear to me that the "Pura Vida" program was becoming well known in the Latino community as students shared and promoted their experiences in the park, and it has exceeded in effectively engaging the community as well.

I was so very proud of this program and our team, and have used it as an example as we seek to engage the next generation of conservation stewards, workforce, and advocates. So, to all of the park staff past and present who created and continue to administer this amazing program—Mary Gibson Scott, Susanne McDonald, Vickie Mates, Megan Kohli,

Vanessa Torres, and Millie Jimenez—my profound thanks for a job well done.

The 2016 Berry Fire was the largest fire in the history of Grand Teton National Park and burned over 20,000 acres in the northern part of the park. I recall the helicopter pilot telling me to return to the fire scene the following year to watch an explosion of elk in the area. To this day, the Berry Fire has been a powerful regenerative force on the park's landscape, and I was so very proud of the brave men and women who were a part of managing it. However, I could not wait for the 2016 fire season to be over!

The Moose-Wilson corridor covers approximately 10,300 acres in the southwest corner of the park and is bounded by the Teton Range to the west, the Snake River to the east, Teton Park Road to the north, and the park's south boundary. The Moose-Wilson Road extends for 7.1 miles through the corridor and serves as the primary access route to several key destinations in the area.

A Draft Plan/Environmental Impact Statement was distributed to the public and other agencies for their review and comment. In response to comments received, modifications and clarifications were made to the plan. Informed by this public input and feedback, and through the phenomenal efforts of our NPS staff and partners, a final decision was reached for the Moose-Wilson Corridor Comprehensive Management Plan in December 2016.

Our nation's national parks continue to serve as popular travel destinations with visitation in 2019 exceeding 300 million recreation visits for the fifth consecutive year. Surpassing 2018 by more than nine million recreation visits, a 2.9% increase, the 327.5 million total is the third highest since record keeping began in 1904. With at least one national park unit located in every state, they offer nearby history, culture, and adventure.

It was a magical experience getting to know the grandson of our founding NPS director. Melissa and I met Stephen (Steve) Mather McPherson, his wife Tina, and members of his family at Jenny Lake Lodge.

We had the opportunity to learn more about their rich family history in the National Park Service, which we continue to value and appreciate today. Steve served and conducted patrols as a seasonal ranger at Yellowstone National Park in the summer of 1958. He entered the private sector, later served on the board of the National Park Foundation, and was chairman of the board of the National Parks Conservation Association, which was founded by his grandfather in 1919. Steve's wife Tina Sloan is an actress who is best known for her role on the CBS daytime drama *Guiding Light* from 1983 until 2009.

I want to take this opportunity to thank my dear friend and predecessor Mary Gibson Scott for her nearly ten years of service as the park's superintendent. With all of the issues and demands that she faced, she truly deserves a well-earned retirement and my sincere thanks for a job well done.

In the late 1970s, and as with many other applicants, I applied for seasonal park ranger jobs in Yellowstone and Grand Teton National Park. I was not successful in landing a seasonal job, but over thirty years later, I would become the superintendent of Grand Teton National Park.

Millie Jimenez with her parents, Grand Teton National Park, 2015, Jimenez Family Photo

Celebrating the NPS Centennial at Grand Teton National Park, 2016, Vela Family Photo

Chapter 18

In addition to majestic landscapes, Grand Teton National Park is home to a wide variety of animals to include grizzly and black bears, bison, moose, and elk. The park advises visitors to always keep a safe distance when viewing wildlife.

Whether in a vehicle or on foot, park visitors must maintain a distance of at least one hundred yards from bears and wolves, and twenty-five yards from all other wildlife. Animals in the park are wild and may act aggressively if approached. Be as knowledgeable as you can by learning about wildlife habitats and animal behavior—always consult with a park ranger—and enjoy your national parks. Unfortunately, during one bear encounter, I myself was less than the required safe distance!

Grand Teton National Park is renowned for hiking opportunities and to have a true wilderness experience. Melissa is the hiker in the family, and valiantly attempted to climb the summit of the Grand Teton. In addition, she joined a group of friends on many hiking excursions throughout the park as well as camped in the backcountry.

The daughter of Mexican immigrants, Millie Jimenez began working at Grand Teton National Park in 2014. Growing up in the Little Italy neighborhood of the Bronx, an internship at Yellowstone National Park solidified her dream of becoming a park ranger. Millie currently serves as the Partnership Coordinator for the C&O Canal National Historical Park located in Washington, DC, and Maryland.

Founder's Day, August 25, 2016, marked the one hundredth anniversary of President Woodrow Wilson's signing of the act that created the National Park Service. Celebrations were held throughout the year with our partners and visitors

L/R Author, Lybby Moore, Laura Fleming, Susan Kingwill, Melissa, and Doreen Wise, Grand Teton National Park, 2018, Vela Family Photo

across the country and at Grand Teton National Park. In addition, the NPS Centennial engaged new audiences and partners, invited everyone to Find Your Park and Encuentra Tu Parque, and strengthened our collaborative stewardship work across the country.

Chapter 19

While performing "Hill visits" as part of my confirmation process, I recall one of my first meetings with a U.S. senator where one of the first questions that I was asked was, "Why do you want to work for this President and administration?" My response was short and to the point: "Senator, he was the first President to ask me to do so." The senator quickly moved on to another subject.

It is important to note that I worked hard within the political arena to build relationships and consensus in order to achieve the interests of the National Park Service. I also worked within and with *all* political interests, which were values that I learned from the late Congressman Mickey Leland of Texas and my parents.

As I was preparing for my confirmation hearing, I asked my dad why we made that trip to Yellowstone National Park. He replied, "Because I wanted my children to experience what my coworkers were saying about their family trip." More than forty years later, his son would be nominated by the President, and provide testimony in order to be confirmed as the nineteenth Director of the National Park Service.

Chapter 20

I had the pleasure of working with P. Daniel (Dan) Smith while he was a special assistant to director Fran Mainella as I was working on a detail assignment in her office. Since that time, we established a long and very valued relationship. Dan first worked in the Department during the Reagan Administration from 1982 to 1986 as Deputy Assistant Secretary for Fish and Wildlife and Parks and as the Director of Legislative and Congressional Affairs for the National Park Service. He then worked in the General Services Administration until 1997 and later became Superintendent of Colonial National Historical Park in Virginia in 2004.

In 2019, I had the honor of addressing the National Association of State Park Directors (NASPD) Conference in Rogers, Arkansas. The conference theme was "Honoring Tradition—Seeking Innovation." Sponsored by the Association of State Park Directors, their mission is to "promote and advance the state park systems of America for their own significance, as well as for their important contributions to the nation's environment, heritage, health, and economy." I greatly valued and appreciated the opportunity to thank my state colleagues for all that they do to protect our nation's heritage as well as to discuss our vision for a second century of service—together.

During a national all-employee call that was held on March 26, 2020, involving the COVID pandemic, I stated, "In my thirty-eight years of public service, I have seen a lot, but have never experienced anything like the challenges we are now facing. And like you, I am relying on the remarkable coworkers around me to ensure that we are doing all that we can to make sound business decisions for our colleagues and the resources entrusted to us by the American people. We are blessed to have in our care some of the most extraordinary places in America. As our nation confronts the challenges of this pandemic, it is these places that remind us of our resilience and shared journey—messages that we all need right now."

Created by President George Washington in 1791, the United States Park Police (USPP) functions as a unit of the National Park Service with jurisdiction in all federal parks. Located in the Washington, DC, New York City, and San Francisco metropolitan areas, U.S. Park Police officers investigate and detain persons suspected of committing offenses against the United States.

Although there are always teachable moments when dealing with demonstrations, to include the events and actions in May 2020, I am very proud of the women and men of the United States Park Police for all that they do to ensure the safe and important expression of free speech for all properties administered by the National Park Service. I was both proud and honored to have worked with them over the course of my career in the National Park Service.

In addition, my special thanks to Jennifer Flynn, associate director for visitor and resource protection, and acting United States Park Police chief Gregory T. Monahan for their leadership and support during the demonstrations held in our nation's capital.

In an email to the NPS workforce entitled "Guiding our Second Century of Service: Washington Support NEXT," I stated our commitment in building a more inclusive environment and transparently sharing the Washington office's vision for a second-century NPS.

I am so very proud of all of our associate directors, regional directors, and staff in the director's office, to include Katie Bliss who served as the acting program manager for NPSNext. With many themes and recommendations that had been put into print over the past decades on a vision(s) for a second-century National Park Service, we had a specific and contemporary blueprint to achieve these interests – within an environment afflicted by COVID.

For over ten years, I had the opportunity to both engage students and leverage capacity in areas of mutual interest with my friends at Clemson University. Lawrence (Larry) R. Allen, PhD—Professor and Dean Emeritus, Department of Parks, Recreation, and Tourism Management; and Brett A. Wright, PhD—Professor & Director, Tigers United University Consortium and Director, Robert H. Brooks Sports Science Institute, are passionate park and conservation professionals. In addition, they are committed to developing the next

Mosaics in Science Interns, Department of the Interior Building, Washington, DC

(L/R) First Row—George McDonald, NPS Youth Program Manager next to the author, (R/L) First Row and far right, Ray Limon, Deputy Assistant Secretary for Human Capital and Diversity, and Chief Human Capital Officer, Department of the Interior, 2020, NPS Photo

generation of conservation stewards with a strong commitment to diversity.

Chapter 21

I began working for the National Park Service during the Reagan Administration and concluded my career in the Trump Administration as a career public servant. In addition, I worked with a number of Administrations of both political parties. I proudly and dutifully served despite any personal differences that I may have had with proposed policies and decisions. One of the best pieces of advice that my parents gave me was to always respect the office that one holds even if you could not respect the officeholder—at every level of government.

Building the next generation of natural resource and visitor service employees, the NPS established the Mosaics in Science Internship Program in 2013. The program provides youth who are under-represented in natural resource science career fields with science-based work experience with the National Park Service. Interns engage in a variety of activities, including research, interpretation, and education projects. Following their internships, a career workshop is held in Washington, DC, where they present the results of their work.

In addition, they are exposed to different science careers and develop skills that are needed in order to apply for a federal job. In partnership with the Environment for the Americas, the program is administered by the NPS Natural Resource Stewardship and Science Directorate and the NPS Youth Programs Division. Whether engaging in a specific program or by volunteering, diverse youth are able to develop social and leadership skills while serving to protect their national heritage.

With a commitment to diversity, and through the interaction with fellow students in historic places, the National History Academy develops students' analytical thinking skills as they evaluate difficult moments in American history while relating those moments to issues that we face today.

Due to COVID, I had the opportunity as acting director to speak to the students virtually on the theme of "Preserving and Presenting American History at America's National Parks." My good friends Bill Sellers, who serves as the President of the National History Academy and the Journey

Through Hallowed Ground National Heritage Area, and Brent Glass, Senior Advisor and Director Emeritus of the Smithsonian's National Museum of American History, are ensuring that current and future generations understand and value the history, law, and government of the United States—by visiting our national parks.

Chapter 22

Our National Park System is to be enjoyed and experienced by all. Every visitor who interacts with the NPS through our parks, programs, and digital media should be able to see themselves in the American story.

As the National Park Service fully embraces a second century of service, it has a unique opportunity to learn from past experiences, mistakes, and achievements in order to prepare the next generation. In the process, we need to ask ourselves, What stories remain to be told, is our workforce reflecting the face of our nation, and what special places are missing within the National Park System?

For many like me, our journey was made possible by ordinary Americans who made extraordinary achievements by standing firm and resolute in ensuring that our national heritage was worth protecting for the use and enjoyment of current and future generations to come. To all of these brave souls both past, present, and future, my profound thanks!

INDEX

Made in the USA
Coppell, TX
14 June 2023

18066796R00142